1

NETWORKING IN THE NEW NORMAL

NETWORKING NEVER LOOKED THIS GOOD...

By

Travis Sims

TABLE OF CONTENTS

Dedication

I would like to dedicate this book to my wife, Dawn Sims, who has been an amazing supporter for all my entrepreneurial ideas. Her unwavering trust gives me the courage to be who I truly am a risk taker in charge of my own destiny.

ABOUT THE AUTHOR

Travis Sims is a Networking Expert, Motivational Speaker, and Thought Leader committed to helping you become a better person, leader, and networker. Travis is a powerful Keynote Speaker engaging audience as large as 3,000 people from all over the world in 49 different countries.

For 14 years Travis was a high-level executive for a global business networking organization breaking records of achievement nationally and internationally.

Travis is known worldwide as the Magician of Networking. He has been teaching & coaching the best business leadership minds across the country how to do networking, build networks, and create community. Travis is the CEO of AGC Accelerated Global Connections the fastest growing business networking organization in the Twin Cities. He is on a mission to help accelerate local business connections in social settings around the world that foster relationships resulting in global opportunities.

Seven years ago, Travis set a goal to lose 100 pounds in one year. He not only accomplished this goal, but he has kept the weight off. Travis has completed some of the toughest competitive Mud Obstacle Courses on the planet, running in the following races: Warrior Dash, Rugged Maniac, Spartan, Battle Frog and the Tough Mudder. Travis enjoys Kickboxing and Martial Arts. He recently earned his blue belt in Kempo

Karate.

Travis believes his success can be attributed to setting goals reviewing them regularly and a strong desire to accomplish them.

CHAPTER ONE

INTRODUCTION

Covid-19, a world-wide pandemic has shaken the world with sickness, loss of life, and crippled the economy with historic unemployment rates and businesses have literally been boarded up for months now. You may be wondering where to go from here, how to advance yourself in business and your career. Ideas on how to innovate and enhance sales in your business may have eluded you lately. You seem to be alone, with no guidance, mentoring, or partnering. Do you feel incapacitated to improve and advance your status and business influence? Opportunities for more jobs and businesses you can do best, seem to fly across your roof, slip through your fingers, and walk right under your nose to your next-door neighbors. They cannot deliver half of what you can do.

Are your clients and customers complaining about a decline in the quality of your product and service? Perhaps you feel like giving up, you have lost every sense of enthusiasm and excitement for your job or business. Have you lost satisfaction with what you do, and what was once precious to you?

Do you think the world is leaving your job, business, or profession behind? Are you speculating that things are no longer the way they used to be, and the corporate world has changed? Do you feel like there's a new normal you haven't discovered yet? Well, I guess you are right. But you are not alone.

I know the reason why you haven't had so much success lately with your business or career. There is a new normal around the world today you have failed to embrace. It is called: NETWORKING. Maybe you think I am bluffing, I guess this mountain of research by Harvard Business School will help you understand better. The investigation revealed that "professional networks lead to more job and business opportunities, broader and deeper knowledge, improve capacity to innovate, faster advancement, and greater status and authority, improves the quality of work and increases job satisfaction."

During the recession in 2008, I had encountered similar problems with my businesses too. I kept on asking myself what I am doing wrong or not doing right. I tried all I could and did all my possible best to do more effectively the same things I have always done overtime to get my business up running again like before, but all my efforts proved abortive. Not until I discovered that the professional or business world has taken another turn. Things have changed. The neglected stone has indeed become the chief cornerstone; networking has become the new normal. Right from that time, I began to see the light at the end of the tunnel. Hope was restored, and having followed the new normal, I eventually bounced back in business. That is why I have written this book to also lead you on the part of discovering and leveraging your network to improve your business or career. This is a New Normal and it evolves again to networking online as the new normal.

I know you must wonder, "what is in for me with this new normal? Can networking help out with solving these problems of mine?" the answer is a big yes! The benefits that accrue when you identify with the concept of networking for your business are innumerable. But, I will give you the tip of the iceberg. Networking is basically about making contact and connection with people of like minds, building a

13

strong and lasting mutually beneficial relationship with them. Hence, you are always ready to assist and, of course, receive help too in times of need.

Putting what networking is all about in mind, you can now see that firstly, networking opens the door for you to create and strengthen long-lasting business relationships. When you continuously reach out to your contacts and always try to maximize every chance to assist them, you are indirectly strengthening the relationship and also paving the way for yourself to receive help in accomplishing your objectives in the nearest future or when you may need it.

Information sharing is another beautiful experience that networking can bring to your doorsteps. It gives you the opportunities to learn new things and new ways of doing old things- something you probably may never have come up with by yourself. If you happen to be on the giving side of the ideas and insight, then you can be sure of building for yourself a strong reputation, respect, and also creating room for cashing out favors sooner or later.

For you to build your career and attract more business and job opportunities, professional networking makes it possible. With your network, you will be able to expand your contacts, make yourself more available to life-changing opportunities, and better job offers at the nick of time.

Networking does not only affect your business or career, but it also affects you. As you keep throwing out yourself to meet and connect with new people, you are building self-confidence for yourself that can profit you in other spheres of your life. You will become bolder to take on new challenges, solve problems, and get more skilled in socialization. As you progress in networking, you also make progress in your ability to create and establish long-lasting relationships.

A great philosopher once told a story about some men who have been trapped in the cave all their lives, they never had a different or clear perspective of other people or other things outside the cave. They only viewed things the way it appeared to them, and not exactly the way they are. One day, one of them got out of the cave, he had experienced the sunlight and seen people and things in another perspective, other than the view he has always had. Dazzled and excited with the discovery, he came back to the cave and announced to the others what he had found. Though they found it hard to believe him initially, when they eventually did, they were able to improve their lives- having a paradigm shift.

Putting the philosopher's story in mind, if you adhere to what I will be teaching you via this book on networking, you will be able to connect with other people in your field of practice, who can introduce to you different perspectives you may not have been exposed to yourself, thereby making your business better and aiding you with prevention abilities to circumvent possible business problems; past, present or future. When next someone tells you that ''experience is the best teacher", don't hesitate to ask the person' ''who's experience exactly? Is it mine or others?'' Wise people don't always allow bad things to happen to them before they can learn. They learn from the mistakes of others, this is the void networking fills.

When you eventually connect wide with professional people using your social media platforms, you can be sure to always find answers to every question that you may have. In cases where there may not be any definite answers for you, you can be sure to receive good suggestions that will help you find better solutions. Also, if you are an employee, then better job offers could come your way through your connections before your contemporaries even find out.

"What will I learn from this book?", you may ask. I will tell you. ''Networking in the new normal'' is a book that will guide you on a step by step approach through the systematic arrangement of the chapters to learn new ways of doing things.

Networking as a professional exercise did not begin in our generation. Since the evolution of business and professional practices, people always had networked. Although, it was not a formally recognized activity like it is today.

Interestingly, the world of business and professional practices are beginning to swim against the tides of the traditional approach to networking. Traditional networking involves a face to face meeting of individuals of like minds, for a mentoring relationship, or to establish a mutually beneficial give-and-take relationship. Corporate events and meetings are sometimes specially organized for this purpose. Different people with different needs come to see what they can offer another to have their own needs met. Some seek to network with others for a recommendation at a better job or to find mentoring, advice partnership... you can fill in the blank spaces.

The challenge with this form of traditional networking is that some people who have the preventive mindset seldom attend these types of meetings; it is disgusting to them. They feel it is full of pretenders, in fact, they consider such meetings as a total waste of time.

Another challenge with this traditional approach for networking is that it leaves little or no room for the shy and introverted to participate. Since you must have to engage another person in a conversation, and not everyone could do this physically on a one-on-one basis, they will end up shying away.

In some other cases, the newbie in the industry will always want to steer clear from such meetings, because they lack sufficient confidence and courage to come around and physically approach high level executives - for them, it is intimidating. Thus, they feel they don't have so much to offer, words to say, and, most importantly, the courage to approach them.

The world is evolving very fast into an absolute digital age. More can now be accomplished with less time, effort, cost, risk, et cetera with the internet and technology. The stress, possible risks, and cost of travelling, the time wastage, energy, and resources consumption to afford the traditional mode of networking started becoming too overwhelming.

Hence, all these challenges I just highlighted above and many more have given rise to a quest for change or an alternative approach to networking. This alternative approach, given that it successfully accommodated the majority rather than the minority the traditional method gathered, making networking (connecting with people) easier, less expensive, less risky, et cetera evolved into becoming a new normal method, and not just an alternative.

People have now learned to appreciate this so-called alternate approach that came as a result of the advent of technology. Today, the use of this approach has seized to become just an alternative, but the new normal. That is why this book is focused on showing you how you can effectively utilize your online presence; the new normal, to make your business thrive, enhance sales, and build professional relationships.

Back to our discussion of what you will learn from this book, firstly, I will start by showing you exhaustively what networking is all about. We will see how that networking simply refers to the interconnectivity of like minds for a sustainable relationship, which will produce a mutually beneficial relationship both in the short-term and in the long-term.

When we are done taking an overview of what networking is all about and how it is a new normal, then I will show you how you can maximize the inherent ability of your connections; a methodological approach to securing high valued connections with people of relevance to you in your field, industry, profession, business and what have you. At this juncture, we will now systematically graduate into exploring the mindset dispositions available for networkers, and which one is right or wrong. The wrong mindset accounts for why a lot of people achieve little or no success in networking. The wrong mindset always looks out for what it can get and not what it can give. We will look at this in detail later in this book. You will not only know what the right mindset for networking would be, but I will also show you how to cultivate it. With the right mindset, you will build strong and lasting relationships that will create profit for you and your business in general.

About half a decade ago, a young professional asked me a question. "How can I be guaranteed of success in my networking as a professional", he said. My response to him was that if you network as a professional, the right ecosystem will determine your success. As for your reading right now, you may also want to ask, "how can I become successful at networking?" my answer has changed from what I told that young man on a Friday eve; "the right ecosystem will determine your success. Thus, in this book, I will be teaching you how to network as a professional in the right ecosystem, and you can be sure of achieving success. I can tell you are already getting excited to know how this is possible- I am as eager to show you.

Connecting with people can be just a connection. But, it's always a different ball game entirely when you authentically connect. An authentic connection will aid you in building a reliable and trustworthy relationship with other professionals. That's not all, I will also guide you through how to make your network-wide, deep, and robust. When your network possesses these characteristics of deepness, wideness, and robustness, it keeps you in the best possible position to cash out the best and first favors available in your industry... I am sure you don't want to miss out on this too.

Have you ever wondered how you can ultimately maximize your time with every connection? Is it possible? Yes! It is. Through the instrumentality of research, which I will show you, you will learn to target the right people, connect with, and consequently how to engage those connections to birth a durable and long-lasting trustworthy relationship and hence, leverage it to increase your sales and maximum productivity.

Mind you, the primary focus of this book is to guide you through every aspect of the new normal of networking. By this, I mean that I will be showing you first-hand how to use the social media platforms available to you to establish professional relationships, build trust, and increase sales or productivity. Therefore, to drive down this point, I will be teaching you how to use LinkedIn, Facebook, Twitter, Instagram, and zoom meetings to network professionally and achieve excellent results.

After you must have successfully learned and applied all of those above, the next line of action would be to multiply value. It is not just enough to learn how to benefit from your relationships, I will also teach you how you can reproduce the value or benefits you already are enjoying or will be enjoying as you follow through with all of what I will be showing you. To multiply the value with your relationships via your network, I will teach you how to reconnect with your contacts, how to access, and activate.

Your network is a powerful tool that can improve your business in general. If you can know how to leverage your network correctly, you can attract more sales, gain more contracts and jobs, access professional advice and mentoring relationships, expand your fame and recognition, get to meet and rub elbows with high level executives et cetera. This is why I will be making known to you the possibilities available to you, and how to capitalize on them to profit your business venture and improve sales.

Many have gotten to the point of establishing connections, trustworthy and long-lasting relationships, and even leveraging those networks for the betterment of their business. But not everyone knows how to maintain the relationship. A lot of people come into networking with the mindset of just to give and take. Like I mentioned earlier, this approach is not always the best, because it will only annul the union in the short term when it seems like there's nothing more to offer momentarily. But, if the relationship was built on trust and sincere concern, it stands the test of time, both parties will benefit and also hope for the best, which is always yet to come. I will also give you some sure basic tips from my fifteen plus years of experience and practice of this technique that will help you sustain a healthy business and professional relationship.

My definition for success does not just mean to prosper at what I am doing, but to see others prosper too. I have realized over time that true happiness comes from helping others become successful in their own ventures in whichever way I can. The joy of every parent is to see their children become better than them or at least to turn out as good as them. I find so much pleasure, satisfaction, and self-fulfilment when I provide guidance and coaching for people, especially in business affairs.

This innate desire of mine to guide and coach people in business has propelled me to write this book. In this book, I will be sharing the experience and expertise I have gathered over time to help you out. At a networking organization known as Accelerated Global Connection (AGC), I coach people and help them establish fruitful connections. I believe that personal relationships drive business. I have observed that secure personal connections often start in a casual environment like social media, outside the traditional workday. The need for productive online meetings and events where people can meet with purpose and begin to do business with people they enjoy hanging out with and consequently become friends, have spurred me to write this book.

If what you are looking for is a Ponzi scheme that will defraud others to give you financial freedom, then maybe at this point, you have to look elsewhere. Perhaps you want a guide that will only teach you how to take advantage of others, exploiting them for your aggrandizement and dumping them afterward, I suggest you stop reading here.

However, if you are that professional, employee or business person as the case may be, who wishes to learn how to be the best at connecting authentically with other business professionals online and develop relationships that will lead to trust and more sales, using social media platforms like: LinkedIn, Facebook, Instagram, Twitter, Zoom meetings et cetera, then you are welcomed to join me further on this journey as I make all your dreams come through. Sit back and enjoy the ride!

CHAPTER TWO
WHAT IS NETWORKING?

Networking is simply marketing; people marketing. A process of engaging others to help you reach your objective. You could say that networking is a simple, cost-effective marketing strategy to position your business out in the Frontline and get meaningful and productive contacts, either based on referrals or introductions, face-to-face meetings at events, or social media connections. The impact of networking on a business or a startup cannot be overemphasized, through networking businesses can increase their reach. In the 21st century, businesses would thrive via networking and collaborations. Business organizations have learned from this pandemic that the world of business is beyond their own distribution chains; with the lockdown of the society and the stalemate of economic activities, business owners have been forced to rethink their business models. They have realized that businesses only doing transactional business will fail and it is businesses that have strong networks that will eventually survive the pandemic. This is the new normal. If your team doesn't know how to network, then you have prepared them to miss opportunities.

Money doesn't stand on its own, money follows people. It is the value you churn out that attracts people to you and in inevitably the money they carry. If you want to make the best out of networking, you need to be sure of what you are offering. Your targets in networking are people.

Networking is the marketing of people.

Networking is a vast concept and cuts across different business endeavours. There is the famous saying; "it's not what you know but who you know. With the situation of the business world today, everyone needs an edge to be at the peak of success. Knowledge profits a lot, but not all. Beyond The knowledge you have, you need the right opportunity and placement to put it to good use, given that many others are just as knowledgeable as you, if not more.

The primary principle guiding networking is common sense; it's that simple. Know what you want and go for it the right way. Behavioural characteristics also matter. Your networks are relative to what you are into as a business professional.

Here are some words to take notice of in networking and building networks;

Process: Networking, as simple a concept as it may appear, needs careful planning and a strategic thought process. It is a voluntary activity that could go wrong if not well thought out.

Engaging: You are hoping to have others look out for you, guide you, give you contacts, recommendations, or introduce you to people that will help your business get better. You will have to convince them to do so. Engage your persuasive and communicative skills, help them see your vision, and be sure they share similar ideas. Have them enthralled and captivated at your first encounter.

Objective: Be clear on why you need to network and why whatever network you are pursuing is important to you. You are not just merely going after networks because you want to try out your acts of persuasion, you must keep it in your consciousness at all times that the sole gain here is business advancement. No one would like to engage someone who isn't clear as to what they wants to achieve in the market space. Also, the clarity as to whom you want to network with, the calibre of people that you want on your team is necessary. You do not want to attract the wrong people that cannot give you the value you need. Networking is powerful only when you know how to use it. You can go about networking the wrong way and only compound parasites for yourself and your business. It is a simple thing, relationships either add or take away from you, so you want to be sure which is which and address the issues.

Where to find: where to find is also something you want to focus on. You do not look for a whale in your backyard, if you want to look for a whale go to where whales swim. It is the same for networking. You want some big catches, you have to go to where they dwell. So, where to find the right network is essential. This is partly why I built my own networking organization AGC Accelerated Global Connections. I found the water shallow in some networks and whales don't swim in shallow waters. Networking is also built with time, you don't want to appear desperate or sinister; you want whoever it is you are engaging to see you as someone first, before they see you as a business person. You want to bring the humanity to your networking, so that the clients can trust you more. Trust is essential in the networking game. So, take your time while building the right community, some might translate into customers, some might work with you, some might be your access to valuable connections, while some would just create opportunities for you, when you have them, nurture them and see your business blossom.

CHAPTER THREE

THE RIGHT MINDSET FOR NETWORKING

According to the Merriam-Webster dictionary, the word mindset could be defined as ''a particular way of thinking: a person's attitude or set of opinions about something''. Further definitions include: "a mental attitude or inclination", "a fixed state of mind". Why a lot of people record failures when it comes to networking, largely depends on their mindset. The attitude or state of mind with which you approach networking would be a major determinant of your success or failure. If you want to succeed in the art of networking, which happens to be the new normal, then you must ensure you possess the right attitude towards it.

You will often hear people complain about how they don't like networking, how that makes them feel uncomfortable. The result of this type of mindset is little or no networking at all, and gathering failures in the few attempts. The primary cause of this kind of thinking rests on the wings of introversion, and networking inspired by a preventive mentality- we will discuss this more in detail later in this chapter.
Scholars in the field of business have done conducted series of research and came up with the conclusion that professional networking with the right mindset produces the greatest success in businesses. Perhaps you are looking forward to having advancement in your business, to

have better and improved knowledge and capacity for innovation, or an enhanced executive presence. Whatever your aim for networking might be, the first step of your one thousand miles begins with having the right mindset. If not, your aim could be frustrated in the long run.

Before I start showing you what the right mindset for networking should be, let me first show you a major mental attitude some people usually adopt for networking that may not yield the best results for them eventually.

WRONG NETWORKING MINDSETS YOU SHOULD AVOID
The first bad mindset I want us to show you is the ''parasitic ideology''. The parasitic ideology in networking shows that the intent one has in networking with other people would be to exploit them or for personal and selfish reasons, and that you do not care about the value that the other person would be getting out of this. The truth is, no one wants to be used or misused. For instance, if you are opportune to connect with someone higher than you in your line of business or industry, which you may not have anything in return to offer, a simple note of gratitude would go a long way to return the favor.

I have realized on several occasions in networking that the people who shy away from networking mostly are those who are still lower on the ladder of achievements in their line of industry. They feel like since they have nothing to offer; hence no need for being parasitic. But wait! This is not always true. Over time, I have come across a lot of high-level executives, who are open-minded to help without prejudice. The right response to this kind of gesture should be to express sincere appreciation and gratitude; this will, in turn, provide the other party with a sense of goodwill, personal satisfaction, and reputation.

Therefore, even in the case of an unequal relationship, you still don't have to be parasitic. It is a very wrong mindset when all you care about is what you will get out of every person you meet with- it is parasitic, and doesn't always end well. I will tell you more about gratitude as we progress.

Psychologists have discovered that one of the predominant mindsets that power networking for some people is the ''preventive mindset''. The preventive mindset speaks of those professionals who feel that there is absolutely no need or pleasure for networking. They consider it a burdensome and an insincere act. Hence, they only engage in it as an act of obligation- achieving little success.

Another important wrong mindset people begin networking with is what I call the '' trade by barter principle''. The trade by barter principle entails that you can only or should only engage in networking solely for transaction purposes, what I can get from you, and what you can get from me. This is wrong! The dangers that abound here is that: firstly, the network won't last long. It won't stand the test of time. This is because it was built on the wrong foundation of 'give and take,' so when there's nothing to give or take anymore at the moment, the whole relationship will go sour. Therefore, as much as lies within you, banish the exchange mentality; the trade by barter principle- it won't take you far.

The second danger of the trade by barter principle is that it doesn't leave you with a good reputation. Since networking is all about people, it means that your dealings with one person could spoil a recommendation for you with another or a criticism. When all you do is give-and-take, you will make people trust you less and deal less with you. This will mean that you will have little success in networking with other people in the long-run.

Let us now proceed to evaluate some of the ways you can cultivate the right mindset for your networking.

CULTIVATING THE RIGHT MINDSET FOR NETWORKING
The first step to take in cultivating the right mindset for networking is preparation. Before you run off to your social media platforms (LinkedIn, Facebook, twitter et cetera) and start conversing with anyone with the intention of building a sustainable network, you have to adequately prepare. Preparation here entails that you do enough research about the person you want to connect with. The essence of the research is to equip you with enough information to initiate a productive conversation.

I know you may want to ask: what if I'm shy and introverted? What if I don't even know how to kick-start the conversation? Well, the solution is to do what you are most comfortable with. Besides the traditional way of engaging someone in a conversation, you can get that person to do it. Simply send the person a beautifully prepared email or message using your social media platforms. The content of your message should be captivating enough, and then the other party could contact you.

Starting a business conversation in networking may not always necessarily be begun on a formal note. You can start with things that you are comfortable with, like sharing a compliment and et cetera; this, however, is not the focus of this chapter, so let's draw the curtain here and continue from where we left off.

Even as you are making preparation to meet your intended partner, making comprehensive research and all, you must also ensure to discover something of mutual interest or your partner's interest- this will be the first sign of selflessness. When you discover what your mutual interest or your potential partner's interest is, it will then equip you with the ability to ask the right questions to establish a good relationship.

Having known the right question to ask, curiosity is what will now give life to the conversation. Never forget that people always want to talk about their favorite subject themselves and themselves all time. Give more attention to focus on what concerns your partner rather than you. Keep displaying curiosity always, ready to learn, and share knowledge. Also, on the thread of preparation, develop an enduring and effective listening skill.

There are so many ways one can pattern their mindset for networking; it could either be right or wrong. The right mindset will always yield the best results in any network you establish. It will guarantee you longevity of your relationships, advancement in your business technical know-how, professional assistance, executive presence, more job opportunities- name them. Networking with the right mindset is indeed, the new normal. The wrong mindset, like I briefly showed you above, will earn you nothing but a temporary benefit and failures in other cases. So, in case you have been networking with the wrong mindset, or you know someone who has, guess what! It's time for a paradigm shift.

I know you may be wondering, "what then is the right mindset?" well, you have nothing to worry about- I've got you covered. Just sit back and tighten your seat belt as I take you on a bumpy ride through the practical mindset that will shape you to get the best out of every network you establish. To help you understand better, I have simplified these necessary mindsets into four. I call them the four SPEG (selflessness, promotion, empathy, and gratitude) of networking mindset. The mindset approach I am teaching you may not sound like the conventional ones you know. Who knows, maybe that's why you haven't had so much success networking. You have been putting your focus on the wrong things. Put your eyes instead on these very simple yet effective networking mindsets, and you will be sure to record success.

SELFLESS MINDSET

Selflessness simply means putting others first before you. When you learn to prioritize the cares of your neighbour before your concern, we can say that you are selfless.

Have you ever come across a hen that wants to protect her chicks from you? Well, if you have ever encountered such, then you would already have an idea of what selflessness is all about. The hen would care less if it would get hurt or anything. It practically gives little attention to its cares, needs, and desires. All it's concerned about is the interest of its chicks.

What about your parents and guardians. You will indeed comprehend the meaning of selflessness when you have been a parent, had a parent or a guardian before. With a zero expectancy ratio in the short-run, a selfless person can make sacrifices and not look back for a payback. I said short-run because, as we will see below, the consequence or benefits of selflessness out rightly outweighs your possible expectations in the long-run.

To be selfless means that you are willing to trade off your time, love, care, resources, et cetera for others, showing true and genuine concern that is motivated by a sense of righteousness and not primarily for yourself interest.

The reason why we must practice the mindset of selfless is that it can never go wrong. You can never be wrong when you put others first. Humans are naturally selfish, so when you bend your instincts to accommodate another person, then you will always be right. Selflessness, therefore, improves your relationship with people.

Selflessness in networking, therefore, entails all I have told you above-this is the right mindset to network with. The mindset of selflessness doesn't just reward you in the future, it provides you with an inner peace of mind, thereby making you feel good and even healthier (scientific discoveries attested to this fact). The effect of this mindset produces gratitude in the heart of the recipient, who will, in return, duly compensate.

Giving that humans naturally love to be valued and appreciated rather than being exploited, your mindset for networking should be primarily based on building a genuine relationship with people as you network. Keep your eyes off, taking advantage of people all the time- it doesn't always end well. People who tend to leverage their relationships or their networks to only obtain advancement will always end up becoming nothing but pretenders. In the long-run, this will always back-fire.

Take my word for it... I have been in business for a long time now, met many people, I have had my successes and failures, but I can beat my chest and tell you that I am a product of networks. Remember the popular saying: '' it is not so much about what you know, but who you know''- this saying is true!

Most often than not, it is more or less a risk when your primary objective for networking is to take advantage of the relationship to get what you want. On the contrary, if you focus on building a natural professional relationship of generosity and selflessness, you will surely reap the fruit of your labor in the long-run.

If you must have trust, faith, reliability, and long-lasting relationships in your network, then you must commit yourself to authentically and genuinely appreciate the other person's values, ideologies, life, work, and goals. You should care beyond work-related matters, make a friend or mentor, and not just a business benefactor. Note that this type of mindset in approaching networking always pays off and does not leave you with a feeling of indebtedness, but of gratitude and appreciation. The mindset of building genuine and honest relationships for networking has overtime proven to be sure, guaranteed, and always successful. Stick with it and thank me later.

To fully absorb this mindset, you have to be willing to put in your energy, your time, and honesty with everyone you come in contact with. No one wants to have anything to do with whom they cannot trust or who does not value and appreciate them.

If you want your network experience to be fun and exciting, then throw away every pre-agendum out from your mind. Focus on building a natural professional relationship. You will always find some excitement along the way when you begin to get favors and other benefits. The end product or consequence of this mindset would outweigh all that you could have ever imagined as a benefit for networking.

There is no one person out there who does not like to be assisted or appreciated. Therefore, your driving factor for networking should be powered by what you can give and not what you can get. Make yourself a helper, try as much as possible to assist, or at least be a listening ear. Don't always look out for what is in it for you; look out for what you can give to another person. A friend of mine would always say: ''What goes around- comes around''. When you create value to people's lives, yours would not be farfetched.

PROMOTIONAL MINDSET
The promotional mindset describes your attitude to want to learn, grow, and thus expand your knowledge and general business or executive presence. You may want to ask: ''what do you mean by executive presence?'' executive presence is an all-encompassing term that explains all the possible corporate or professional dealings associated with an individual concerning their industry of specialization.
The promotional mindset is fuelled by curiosity. This mindset type erases the selfish mentality and keeps you on your toes to always observe and watch out for the interest of your partner while you learn and grow. You must be wondering: isn't this selfishness in its self? Are you not being selfish by desiring to leverage the relationship to learn and grow? The general answer is a big fat, no!

Adam smith: a renowned economist. He is regarded as the father of economics by many scholars. In one of his theories- courtesy of his phenomenal book ''an inquiry into the nature and wealth of nations'', he explained that when people pursue their selfish aims, they will end up achieving the societal interest in the long-run. However, in the context of what we are discussing, not every personal aim leads to the benefaction of all in the long-run. The one personal aim you can pursue here that will lead to the general good of all would be 'knowledge and growth' why? Because when you want to learn, you will be curious to ask. And when you are curious to ask, you will be eager to listen.

When you become a good listener, you are already prioritizing the cares and concerns of the other party over yours and boom! You are learning. People will always want to talk about themselves; they feel valued, loved, and appreciated when you hear them out and understand their ideologies. Hence, when they feel this connection, the relationship solidifies more. You will now agree with me that the promotional mindset- through sounds counterproductive yields tremendous results for your networking experience.

EMPATHY MINDSET

In the Hebrew culture, their leaders are always told to love and treat their neighbors as they would love to be treated themselves. In our discussion of an appropriate networking mindset, I want you to note that this ideology holds a lot of water. By the empathy mindset, you are meant to treat others how you want to be treated. I strongly believe nobody wants to be exploited; nobody wants to be used and dumped. I am sure you would not appreciate it if someone just chats you up on a social media platform, and the first thing they ask is for you to introduce them to your CEO – you will not be comfortable with that, right? So why do you do this to others? Perhaps, if you had approached that business connection the way you would have loved to be approached, then you may have established a beautiful relationship already.

Empathy is a crucial networking mindset every networker must possess. I believe if we all deal with one another empathically, peace will always reign, hurt will vanish, and a generous, sincere and genuine network of faithful people will thrive, thereby making the professional world a better place.

Upcoming entrepreneurs who have little or nothing to offer are always scared of approaching the high-level executives. Some are shy, and others are sceptical or scared of how they may be treated. Just imagine that the norm of networking mindset is empathy... wow! Your guess is as good as mine; everyone's professional needs would be met. People can now summon enough courage to approach their potential referral partners without fear- what a happy story networking will tell. Think about it!

GRATITUDE
An ungrateful person will only end up a great fool. Ungrateful people will

always fall short from any relationship or network they try to establish. On the flip side, beyond the general concept of thanking someone after a job well-done, gratitude in networking has bridged the gap between highly decorated executives and beginners. That is, for those who don't have much to offer, a mind that is set on thanksgiving and appreciation balances the equation. Whether you get anything in return or not, never stop saying ''thank you''- it does a lot of magic. Try it out and find out for yourself.

Conclusively, to effectively and efficiently leverage your networks and get ahead in life and business, the right mindset is to focus on the people rather than what they have to offer. When you secure a connection with the people, what they have to offer will naturally come to you.

CHAPTER FOUR
NETWORKING FOR PROFESSIONALS

You already have a knowledge of what "networking" is and the right mindset to have in networking. Now let's advance a bit and talk about "Professional Networking." Professional Networking can simply be defined as networking focused on achieving professional goals. It is a deliberate activity that professionals engage in to build, strengthen, and sustain relationships of trust with other professionals to advance their businesses and achieve their goals. A good network plays a huge role in exposing you to knowledge that you need to make progress in your profession. Building relationships that are founded on trust is very essential in professional networking. It is not enough to pitch a sales or swap business cards and leave the other person thinking that the relationship is solely about business benefits, that you are taking advantage of an opportunity, or that you are using them to achieve your professional goals. You must make sure that you do not sell your intending network the idea that you are connecting with them for selfish reasons. For networking to be truly effective, real relationships must be built. Relationships that are not one-sided or parasitic, but rather mutual relationships that are beneficial to both parties. A relationship that adds a lot of value to each person.

REASONS TO ENGAGE IN PROFESSIONAL NETWORKING.

Professional Networking has become incredibly popular in the business world. Businesspeople, engineers, lawyers, content creators, etc. all have networks that offer them a good value. People engage in professional networking for some reasons, including:

ACCESS TO INFORMATION AND HIGH-QUALITY KNOWLEDGE

Professionals understand that there are things you can't just know by reading alone. You need people who have done it before who have the experience and the knowledge that they can pass on to you only if you can engage with them on a personal level. Information is expensive. It is power, and it is precious. Building a network of experienced and knowledgeable people in a given field can be a huge boost for any professional in that field.

TO BUILD A PERCEPTION

You can engage in professional networking when you want to establish yourself as an expert in a given field. By giving high-quality knowledge and information to your network, you take a top spot in their minds. When they think of your profession, you are the first person that will come to their mind.

TO BUILD NEW PROFESSIONAL RELATIONSHIPS OR STRENGTHEN EXISTING ONES

No one person is an island. You need credible relationships if you want to succeed in a chosen endeavour. The era of one-person-team is gone. This is the era of collaboration. Your professional relationships can come in handy during periods of crisis or hardship. Build professional relationships, and don't forget your old relationships. People tend to forget existing relationships when they begin to build new ones. Don't make that mistake. Never forsake a relationship that is of good value to you. You may only shoot yourself in the foot.

TO BUILD TRUST

Like we stated earlier, networking can only be effective when the relationship is built on trust rather than for solely selfish business reasons. Building a professional network with other professionals can help increase their trust in you and your brand and will also help you trust them and their brand.

TO HAVE A GOOD TIME

This is a good reason too. Work can get stressful, and one of the ways to shake off the stress is to meet with your network and have a fun time. You could have a conversation over coffee or lunch, or you could go for a walk. It is a relationship, remember? It is not just for business reasons. Having a good time can also help you build trust in your relationship, and that will do a lot of good to your professional life as well. People don't always remember all the details but they remember how they feel when they're with you.

TO PROMOTE YOURSELF AND YOUR BRAND

You can also engage in professional networking to promote yourself and your brand. Nobody will know what you do if you don't talk about yourself. Spreading knowledge of yourself and what you do is a good way to ensure that you take top spot in people's minds. Talk about who you are and what you do. You can even take it a step further by talking about how you do it and what you hope to achieve by doing it.

THE RIGHT ECOSYSTEM WILL DETERMINE YOUR SUCCESS

ECOSYSTEM - this term has become very popular. People use the term now and then without even thinking about the implications that the word holds. Many times what people refer to as an "ecosystem" could be a toxic environment that is harmful to business success.

Professional Networking is a necessity in business, and you must build one with the right ecosystem in mind. The right ecosystem consists of three very important facets. These include:

CAPITAL: Businesses are built and sustained by capital. No business can thrive without money and pertinent infrastructure. Build your ecosystem and ensure that you build the right network individuals that can help you to raise enough capital if you ever need to finance a business or a project.

KNOW-HOW (SKILL): The right ecosystem will also consist of professionals with the skills and technical knowledge required for launching and growing a business. Build a network of professionals with the skills you need, this can provide you with the workforce for recruitment.

INNOVATION: Lastly, innovation is the nutrient-rich food that makes a business thrive. Your business will remain average if you stick to the status quo. Dare to be a creative rebel. Break the generally accepted codes and set new ones. However, do it intelligently. Your professional network or ecosystem can play a massive role when it comes to innovation. Build a network of innovators and "outside the box" thinkers who will drive your business to the next level.

HOW YOUR NETWORK CAN DETERMINE YOUR SUCCESS.

No one can deny the kind of impact that a successful professional network can make in your career. Most experts will agree that the most connected people are the ones who are most successful. Don't underestimate the role that your network plays in your success. When rightly executed, networking can give you the competitive edge that you need to achieve awesome results in your career. Most people will say that success is a combination of talent, hard work, and luck. But I will substitute luck with the word network. Yes, luck is required in getting the right exposure and awesome opportunities, but you can leverage your network to create your luck. Many successful people today will tell that the reason why they are where they are today is major because of the role that successful networks played in their career development. Many people are not so talented, but they are more successful than other very talented people because of the professional connections that they have managed to build over time. I am not saying that you should throw talent in the trash can. You still need the talent to succeed; after all, if you don't have any talent, then you have nothing to offer. But your network increases your odds of success. Your network offers you the opportunity to emerge and show what you can offer. If you are starting up a new venture, your network offers you capital, knowledge, skillsets, partners, and so much more.

Networking on a professional level is highly essential if you want to advance in your profession. It gives you access to valuable information and high-quality knowledge on a level that random and close friends, relationships, or acquaintances cannot provide. It also exposes you to diverse opportunities that can help you build a credible brand while making more money. Here are some ways that professional networking can help you advance your career and contribute to your overall success.

AVENUE TO LEARN

Your professional network can offer you the opportunity to learn and discover new ideas that you never knew could be applied. It can expose you to high-quality knowledge that can lead to a much-needed innovation in your career or company. Business knowledge is an essential asset to any businessperson. It is a collection of all the experience, facts, know-how that you have gained over years of work. Now, you don't need to work too long to get the knowledge you require to advance your business. All you need is a rich pool or network with the required knowledge and experience that you can learn from and apply to your own business.

INCREASED SALES

All you might need to jump from fifty sales to five hundred sales could be just one word from your network. Earning the trust of your professional network and getting them to promote your products or services can boost credibility and sales. Sales are essential in building loyalty and trust with customers. The more sales you make, the more your customers will trust your brand, and the more they will recommend your products to potential customers. A recommendation is highly valued by prospects because it is coming from a third party who is not attached to the business and hence carries more credibility.

TALENT FOR RECRUITMENT

If you have never been in dire need of a particular skill set to carry out an urgent project that requires expert handling, then you might not know the value of having individuals with diverse skill sets and experts in different fields within your reach. Your network can expose you to a rich plethora of individuals with diverse skill sets that are readily available for recruitment. Not only will these boost the quality of your work force but will enable you to carry out important projects quickly in the most expert fashion.

COMMON INTEREST

Building a professional network will allow you to meet individuals who share the same interests with you. This can lead to high-income collaborations in the future. One very important factor that contributes to the success of any business is teamwork. Working with a team enables people to be faster in carrying out their tasks as well as be more effective in achieving their goals as compared to people who work on their own. Two heads are better than one. When two highly talented and knowledgeable people combine their skills and knowledge to achieve a common goal, the result is always tremendous. Collaboration allows the parties involved to complement one another's and make up for one another's weaknesses while enhancing their strengths. Collaboration is the juice that every business craves for, and your network can offer highly qualified teams to collaborate with.

HIGHER SOCIAL STATUS

The saying, "birds of the same feather flock together," could never be truer. Mingling with high-quality individuals will automatically make you a high-quality individual. Every professional craves for a high social status as this allows you to influence major decisions in society. It also enhances your credibility and gives your audience a big reason to trust your brand. However, ensure that the relationship is not a parasitic relationship where you are the only one benefitting from their social influence. Remember, networking is truly beneficial when the relationship is built on trust. Make sure you are adding value to the other person's life as well, and they will see you as a truly honest individual who is not in their lives only to benefit from their high social status.

ACCESS TO TOP SOCIAL EVENTS

Social events are very important. It not only allows you to take a break from a very strenuous workload and catch some air, but it also exposes you to new knowledge and ideas. It allows you to socialize, meet new people, and let people know you. Watching people talk about themselves and what they do can be a huge motivation for you. You may even get to meet someone who can offer you a solution to a problem you are facing. Having a rich network of professionals can allow you to attend the top social events both inside and outside your business circle. Events that you normally will not be invited to, if not for the connections that you have and the strings you can pull. Attending these events further exposes you to other professionals both in your sphere of business and outside your sphere of business. People you can network with to build a strong network that promises to be useful in the future.

BRAND VISIBILITY

Your network can also go a long way in promoting your brand and increasing your visibility. You could get the opportunity to come to talk about what you do at social events that will increase your marketing reach and boost your sales. You could get invited to public speaking events as a speaker or trainer for a fee or for free, which can further promote your brand. Every entrepreneur knows how important brand visibility is. Brand visibility helps you keep your brand top-of-mind with your audience. Brand visibility helps people know what you offer and how valuable your product is. Your network can help make your brand visible and hence increase your audience, build brand affinity, and increase website traffic.

NEW OPPORTUNITIES AND VENTURES
You will not know how much you know or don't know until you have a conversation with someone. Every businessperson must be open to new opportunities. What product or service does your venture not have that the market craves for? How could you grow your business to make your products more affordable and allow more customers to patronize you? Opportunities abound, but you may not see any if no one shows you. Your network can expose you to diverse opportunities and ventures - you never knew existed - that will give you a much needed financial boost.

HOW TO BUILD AND MAINTAIN YOUR PROFESSIONAL NETWORKS
Building a professional network is not the most difficult thing to do. You just have to be willing and eager to engage in those small talks that most people are scared of. You must be willing to make an extra effort if you want to build a rich network that will help you advance your career and expose you to valuable opportunities.

BE PRESENT AT EVENTS
Jump at every opportunity to attend online or in person social or networking events organized for the kind of people you need to meet to advance your career and change your life. These events will offer you the opportunity to meet new people and build a mutually beneficial relationship with them. Since the new normal is online, be ready to attend online events; get a good router that ensures fast and hitch-less internet access so that you don't show up, but you show up prepared.

BE ACTIVE
Learn to be outgoing. Even if you are an introvert, always give yourself a good reason why you should meet new people. If becoming financially

free is not a good enough reason for you, then find one good enough reason for yourself. Be willing to have conversations with people you just met and don't just stay still listening to them, actively engage in the conversation, and share your views. Most people claim that the reason why they feel reluctant about engaging in conversations with new people is that they don't have anything to say. Well, I think they have a lot to say, but don't know how to start the conversation. You can learn a few starting statements to kick off conversations. You can say something like, "my name is Travis, how are you?" Follow up with an open-ended question. Open-ended questions are questions that they can't answer with a yes or a no. These will allow you to advance the conversation and have more things to talk about. Some open-ended questions you can use include: "How did you hear about this event?" "What did you take away from the presentation?" "What do you do?"

SHARE YOUR KNOWLEDGE

Don't be afraid to share your knowledge with the people you meet. First impressions matter a lot, and most times, the first impression you leave with a new contact will determine the course of your relationship. The best way to impress someone you are meeting for the first time is to offer them your valuable knowledge. They will see your connection as something that will be very essential to them in the future, and they will love to learn more from your wealth of knowledge. But be careful so that they do not think that you are a stuck up person who just likes to show off. Let them see that you really, and genuinely care about using your knowledge to strengthen their businesses or better their lives.

FOLLOW UP

This is a very essential part of networking that professionals always overlook. The first contact you make with an individual is useless and a waste of time if you fail to follow up. You do not have to set up a dinner meeting with them the next day or send a long emotional text. But you can follow up by sending them a connection request on LinkedIn, AGC or sending a friend request on Facebook. You can even have a quick phone call to ask them how they are doing. By doing this, you are slowly building a connection with them, and this connection will lead to a valuable network that you will find useful in the future.

STAY RELEVANT

Don't fail to remain relevant to your networks. Learn new things and share relevant knowledge with them. Keep up-to-date with recent trends and valuable information that your networks will find useful. Don't give in to the temptation of asking them for help immediately. Find opportunities to offer them value now and then. Being valuable to your network will help you earn their trust and increase your chances of not being turned down when you finally ask for help in the future.

CHAPTER FIVE
HOW TO CONNECT AUTHENTICALLY; MAKE YOUR NETWORK WIDE, DEEP AND ROBUST

B uilding a robust network can be easy and difficult at the same time, depending on the kind of principles you decide to apply. Most of the time, people always run off with a cliché, "hard work is everything," but often, at times you will notice that even when you decide to work hard in the wrong direction or with the wrong tools, you will notice that you will come out with little or no results. Some right methods and tools can be rightly put into effective use that will boost your network, and they can help you in achieving your desired result as far as business networking is concerned.

In this chapter we will look at some of the principles and tools we can rightly apply that will give us the right results and they are as follows:

HELP PEOPLE
Humans are more attached to people that offer help or offer solutions to their problems. So on the onset, have it in mind that the fastest and easiest way to build a tangible business network is to be a solution to people and do it in such a way that it seems you are doing it for free.

These solutions can be seen in the form of business ideas, inspiration, motivation, links on where they can get loans for their businesses, that is, if you are not in a proper situation to do that. See it as offering value to people in exchange for their attention.

The world seems to be getting extra business with tons of things and people battling for people's attention, so if you are going to gain people's attention, you have to do it in such a way that your product, service or help is more valuable than what they can get out there on the streets.

BUILD YOUR SMART LISTS
Communicating with your network is quite vital and can be fun, especially when working with social media, but have you ever thought of how you can communicate with them if probably your social media handle gets hacked or for some unknown reason you lose all your contact on socials. A wise businessperson or even someone who wants to run a personal brand would have to build a standard list of their network. I know it might sound odd to directly ask your clients to send you their details, but there could be other ways to make this professional. You can use the cheese and the mouse system of which most strong brands are using now to build their network list.

First, you will understand that "there is no free lunch in London." You will have to create a Google Form with the right questions attached and lure them with a free webinar, a good book, or another thing promising, but be sure to stand by your word, most customers tend to trust brands with a good record of proven integrity.

BE CONSISTENT WITH THE RIGHT CONTENT
Content is probably like the main cookie in the cookie jar. Employing the power of the right message in communicating with your audience will go a long way to keep them loyal to you. The right content will have to communicate the right emotions since humans are quite sympathetic. However, there are some that have decided to explore the power of logical reasoning in every matter; you will have to feed them with the right content too. So you will have to explore the power of storytelling in conveying sympathy and empathy.

This should be the norm of your social media handle updates, your newsletter, and other forms of updates. This will have to involve trends, action points, the right graphics, and every other thing that will appeal to human reasoning. But you have to be professional in your approach, so people don't see you as an opportunist.

Content has to speak to people's needs starting with what the people/ world is facing; economic crisis, pandemic, religious celebrations, and the rest, and the only possible way you can get access to people's information on their beliefs, business scope and what they're possibly facing is from your list building system. This is more like taking a course on human resource management and human relations at the same time, but these core areas need to be put into due consideration.

Another thing note-worthy with regards to content is to master the art of storytelling, which would capture the attention of your audience. Effective mastering of this art puts you on edge in trying to pass along your message. It has been proven that capturing the attention of humans in today's busy world would have to be done within the first few seconds of communication, and within that little time frame, the content should be quite engaging so that the person receiving the content gets interested.

GO PERSONAL

Clients don't want to be seen as just every other person on the street that receives newsletters in their email or receives a text on every normal day. Everyone craves for attention in one way or the other. If you are going to win the hearts of your clients and new clients, you will have to treat them like they are unique.

So how do you get to do this considering the number of people you might be dealing with? Still boils down to email marketing and Google forms. The forms should be prepared in such a way that it captures their first name or nickname. People tend to feel unique when you address them by their name. More so, try and communicate with them privately on social media but do not neglect to make it professionally informal.

In some cases, it is advisable to have a physical meeting in most cases. And this would lead you to build actual connections with people and not just see it as a mechanical relationship or a give and take relationship, exploring empathy and sympathy in your networks. So, phone calls, personal texts, private chats, customized messages in situations where you are extremely busy can go a long way against the regular broadcast messages, and social media feeds.

ATTEND ONLINE MEETINGS

Social gatherings and online meetings are good places to meet new people and authenticate already existing networks. So you will have to step out of your room or office and attend online social gathering, online meetings, and much more, especially when you are sure you would meet someone that you are looking for.

At such an online event, you would have to take note of a few things that can count in aiding you to meet and maintain the right contacts. First, you should introduce yourself to people and not wait for them to talk to you. This has a way of showcasing your boldness and confidence in your abilities and your interest in people mildly and appealingly. People would have to be sure you are confident in your abilities, and you are interested in them.

The next is to find common ground for a good conversation; it does not need to be all about work, most people are stressed out about their jobs, and they want to cool off from the cooperate world and appear a bit informal. You can start with complimenting their looks, picking out one thing you like about them, and complimenting them, and this should not be mistaken for cheap flattery. More so, your conversation should not be boring and one-sided; you would have to be smart in your conversation and keep it rolling like a tennis ball; from one side of the court to another.

Then move to other people when you have established contact with them. Staying with one person can make you look like a pest in such meetings. This should be done in such a way that they don't see you as a gold digger and do well to communicate with them after the event; maintain such communications and be sure not to pester people.

Connect with clients and those you've met at online events or training on LinkedIn – by writing personal notes, not just simply relying on the standard " I'd like to connect" messaging provided by the platform. Learn to pay keen attention to your social media replies and be sure to show genuine connection though your personalized messages. This should be done within at least 48 hours of meeting such people, so your memory doesn't become vague and more so try and follow up the process.

BUILD A VISIBLE REPUTATION
In working in the corporate world, you would have to have built a reputation over time. If people are going to trust you to network with

you, then they would have to see you as someone credible and genuine in your line of work.

This would give people a reason to trust you, and your credibility should be smartly visible on social media in a way that it does not look like a threat but should smartly be positioned in a way that people see you helping others and would want you to help them too.

Reputation and visibility should go hand in hand to help in attracting the right networks your way; that means you should be Google-able. Google is the largest search engine, and most people tend to go on Google in search of new things, and on searching for possible solutions, there should be links on how to reach out to you with your achievements and reputation visibly present.

Post periodic updates on LinkedIn (heck it is a great place to share the firm's newsletter, industry alerts, and upcoming speaking engagements). Through this, people would seemingly follow you, especially if there are provisions that would accommodate them.

USE THE POWER OF TECHNOLOGY

With the growing trend in technology, people tend to depend less on physical meet-ups to build their network but more on what technology has provided like the Zoom meetings, cloud meet-ups, and the rest. The average individual who wants to network will possibly use the power of technology to explore easier ways of reaching you. So be sure to give them that opportunity when the time comes.

This also involves exploring the power of technology in trying to communicate effectively with your clients and your network line. Zoom meetings, organizing Instagram live sessions, Facebook live sessions, exploring digital marketing skills, all should be within your reach in trying to communicate with and maintain effective communication with potential clients and already formed networks effectively.

This should be structured in such a way that it does not contradict the aforementioned principles. Try as much as possible to communicate with everyone at his or her level.

BE UPDATED

People would want to communicate well with someone they know is constantly improving themselves and growing, especially in relation to new things. There are respect and reputation naturally attached to people who take steps to improve themselves.

With your growing improvement, people tend to be more attracted to you and be sure to update such achievements and improvements to your LinkedIn profile, web pages, social media profiles, and the rest. More so, offer to show people how they can be like you and achieve more in everything they are doing. By doing so, they see you as successful, and with your hand stretched out to help them, they would come to you.

THINK LONG TERM
Most of the time, because people are strategic in their networking patterns, they tend to focus actively on limited networks that will offer them the solution to what they need and shut out the rest, only to remember them when the need arises again. This could be seen as strategic, but in the long run, this only hurts you because the already built networks would not trust your network. They would only see you as someone that comes to them when you are in need.

Therefore, constant communication can be seen as a key to maintain already existing networks and serve as a path to new ones. People would have to link up to other people to you due to the trust and constant communication. Link ups are one of the fastest ways to broaden your network without sweating that much, just living your life, enjoying the current relationship while the network works on expanding the network for you.

More so, in some business situations, think of collaborations instead of running off on your own with new ideas and looking out for help from others. Often times, people do not want to compete with anyone and would see potential competitors as threats. In such cases, they fight off potential partners and may damage their businesses for life because they might pick a fight with a big corporation that may go all out to take them out of business. Business collaborations can also expose you too new networks that you can savour to build new networks.

BUILD A BRAND SIGNATURE:
As a corporate body of even as an individual, it is vital to consciously build your brand. This means that you consciously build the perspective

you want your friends, clients, colleagues, and potential networks to see you as. In doing this, you would have to pay close attention to some elements that represent your business outside.

Business logos, your chosen colors, and other elements must be properly set in place. This will always reflect on how you send your newsletters, reply texts, package your voicemail, etc. and this, in turn, affects how already existing customers see you and will go a long way to tell if a potential network would want to connect with you or not.

MINORS BUT VERY IMPORTANT:
There are quite some other points worthy of noting that are quite little in view but mean a lot in trying to build your network and make it robust. Some of such includes:

Regularly review and update the bio you have provided for inclusion on the firm's website and seek out opportunities to contribute to the firm's newsletter. These constant updates make people aware that you are actively involved in the company's growth if you are not the one in charge of the business. It also makes people know that if they are willing to reach you through the company's website that you are sure to respond in a timely manner.

Contribute your thought-leadership to industry publications (to give your expertise a higher chance to benefit from word-of-mouth referrals). Things like magazines, research materials, and the rest are materials that could go viral, especially among closely related industries. Contributing actively to such substances can create an avenue of publicity for you and make people be on the lookout for you. Even when they do not start up the networking line, it serves as a good credibility point for you. People can leverage on that and see you as an expert in your industry.

Check the bio you use for awards and/or speaking activities – and consider customizing it for each request. This has a way of telling people that you are organized and do not take the awards as the ultimate in life but see it as an avenue to reach further for higher goals.

Ensure your headshot is current – regardless of how good you looked when your career started or how much you hate having a picture taken. Funny enough, but constantly reviewing your headshots gives people something new to look out for when they visit your website, LinkedIn account, or your social media profiles. This can get them engaged and invariably spark up conversations.

Create and grow your holiday card or E-card mailing list. This would be seen in the way you send such cards during holidays. Be sure to hand –sign physical cards that would be sent to your clients. They would not just see it as a card from the company; they would see it as a personal extension of love and care.

Revise your not-for-profit board profile or bio (if you sit on one of these boards) to highlight more than simply your passion for the cause. Boards are a chance to diversify your network -recognize it and take advantage of it. More so, people would want to relate with people that are readily interested in humanitarian projects because they would want to see that you care genuinely for mankind and, at such, would want to connect with you possibly to organize more of such projects or for business purposes.

Complete and/or update your membership profile on any professional organization, industry, and/ or alumni directories. This should be taken as very important; most contacts and connections are such that come from forms filled in occasions, a business meeting in some cases training courses. These contacts lookout for some necessary details in trying to connect and may, in turn, communicate with you.

More so, old-time classmates might want to connect and do business for old time's sake, so filling out the alumni board documents can go a long way to make your contacts available for such.

Review your business card information from time to time, especially if the scope of your business is broadening. Add some new look to it too from time to time, but keep the brand signature in check to avoid losing your brand perception except for when you want deliberately do so.

Be prompt in responding to messages and voice mails. Set Google alerts for key clients or targeted industry happenings as being the first to send a "congratulations message on the new role or just read that..." email will solidify a connection. The message craft should not be all formal if you want to strike a chord in the memory of your clients.

53

Remember, the primary thing is to be visible and easily relatable with people. Putting yourself in a situation where people can access you readily without much stress can be one of the most priceless things to note in trying to build your business network. This will, in turn, make the networks you have built authentic and robust, which you can leverage on to build a successful business.

CHAPTER SIX
RESEARCH

To make the right connections, one of the steps you have to take is to do your research on the kind of connections you want to make. Research your connections and know as much about them as you can. Before you finally meet and make that connection you want so much, preparing for it is what will save you from blowing that opportunity when the opportunity finally comes. Research is how you learn about your potential connections and network and prepare to have the right kind of conversation with them when you finally meet them. That is how you prepare to make your impression, and stand the chance of winning them over.

Preparation is the key with which you beat the unknown, research is equal to preparation in this case. When you finally meet them, you will have known what kind of conversation they like to get into, what their business is about, all the things that interest them, and how they think. Do your homework on them, don't just sit and expect that things will simply take place and turn out in your favor, or that when you land the opportunity to make a connection, you will nail it without preparing for it. The truth is, things don't work like that, and you may just be taken by surprise.

Coming by business relationships and a network that is beneficial is not always easy. What that simply means is that it will not always happen the way it does with meeting and making new friends every other day. This is a business network, and the opportunity does not always come that easy, neither is building a relationship. Remember, business owners are looking for who will add value to them and their business, and unless you are that person, they may not want to waste their time.

One way to know what a certain business relationship is interested in, and how to connect with them is through research. Get to know everything possible about each target business. I will say this again, do your homework before you start trying to have that network you are looking to have. This will go a long way for you when you eventually come by those relationship opportunities. Let this sink in as deep as possible. You need to get to know the people or person you want to meet before meeting them. Whether that is online or physically. By the way, people and businesses mostly meet and connect on social media platforms way before they ever meet physically.

You may still be wondering how that matters, well it does matter a great deal, and just so you know again, this is probably the only way you get to know how to appeal to them.

There is a saying that goes like this," busy people attract busy people," and that couldn't be farther from the truth. If you are in the business world seeking to connect and make relationships with business people like you, you stand a chance because you all speak the same language—business. But even if you weren't a business person, so long as you have something to offer, something that can be of value, you will have a chance. The most important thing, however, is to know enough to have good and memorable communication with that individual when you meet them.

Doing your research will prepare you to meet your potential network with good, valuable, and appealing content. So do your research, get to know your connection, and prepare to leave an unforgettable impression on them. When you do your research, you will almost not have a question to ask about them. That may sound like a horrible way to make a connection, but it may well be a good one instead. Imagine how you will feel if you were approached by a fellow businessperson who seems to know so much about you and what you do that they do not have to ask what you do. This will leave an impression of importance; it will leave you feeling like your business is doing well as the person cares about what you do. It's a good way to begin a relationship. You don't have to answer some questions.

TARGET MARKET

No one ventures into a business without thinking of who that business is going to benefit, in fact, the "who" the business is going to benefit would determine the "what", and "where" of your business; and even greatly influence the "why". Here is what I mean, the people you are servicing would determine what service you would design, they would also determine, how this service would be delivered and to where it would be delivered. That means, your market determines for a smart marketer, your business. Now that almost all of the world is online, it would be crazy if any business is not seeing how they can leverage the new market. So, you build your target with that in mind. You know that your target market would help you crystalize your idea and would determine how that product would function in the market.

So first, you will have to identify the category of business persons whose acquaintance you will love to acquire and pay attention through research to the different kinds of networking chances that will easily touch them. If you can nail this down, then you will be on your way to making that connection happen.

To make the most out of your target market when you eventually meet them, you will need to have something to present. Networking online, you may discover, is a bit more difficult than networking offline. A lot of physical factors will play a support role for you. For example, the way you look, the way you sound, the way you talk, even the way you smell. Making offline connections are quite advantageous in the sense that your prospect can see you and make a physical connection with you. Nothing, always, beats connecting physically.

Because of this, in targeting your prospect, you, too, should make sure that you are ready for that network connection when you finally come by it. Now very important when targeting your prospective network is the need to be in the right place—the right online community. To do this, you need to first understand what your niche is and be sure you do not confuse your prospect. Define your brand and business and use that definition to target your prospect. Find the community in which your desired network is found and build a presence and influence there. Make yourself known and actively follow these prospective network personnel.

Go to your market audience, look for other influential business members there, and start following them. It is through this that you will begin to do your research about these influential members and build a good foundation based on knowledge, for a possible relationship.

Networking online is as easy as being active enough to understand what is going on and how things are done in a given business community. Aim your target well enough and prepare to connect with them eventually, because the opportunity will come.

Google provides an easy and simple way to connect and engage with the right community and network of people as you need, depending on what your business or market is. Through the use of a Google networking platform, you can reach your target network, and they can reach you as well. All you need to do is simply find the right social platform and set up your profile to attract and be found by your target network. So build up your profile to be easily attractable to similar profiles using almost all social media, online platforms.

Leverage your strength and use it as a visibility technique to draw your network target market to yourself. By all means, possibly online, seek to be seen and known, but mostly in the right online environment. In other words, make yourself and your business visible to the right community—the very type of prospect you want to create and build a business and networking relationship with. This does not imply reaching out to everyone in an online community, but rather, seeking out those specific prospects with whom you should have a relationship with.

Lastly, there are forums in which you would find online, professional business people who are likeminded. AGC, Facebook, Instagram, Twitter, LinkedIn, Google, and lots of other online platforms out there have easy ways of suggesting and connecting you with people who are similar to you professionally. This makes it easy to target, engage, connect, and build a good relationship with whoever appeals to you. The truth is, all these business owners are equally looking for how to connect with other similar business people and build a good and trustworthy relationship that will benefit both parties. Everyone is looking for the right people to network with, just be sure to bring something you can offer in exchange for their value.

CONNECT

A connection is where a relationship is determined or not determined. It is your strengths that will play a good role in helping you connect with your prospect when you get talking. Before professionally engaging a new business relationship you just made, you have to make a connection first. Because it is a business relationship first, you need to be able to appeal to the business person through proving your relevance or the relevance of your "business"—relationship to them.

With the help of the research you should have done on your prospective relationship and positioning properly, you should be able to pull through this phase. The connection stage is where communication happens, fostering a good interaction between you and this new network of a business relationship. Some of the best business platforms where you can easily find and make connections with the right business professionals, especially as a new business owner online, are AGC, Facebook, Twitter, Instagram and LinkedIn. You can utilize these platforms and maximize your time in each of them. Maximization begins with the way you set up your profile. The next will be who you follow and your interests. This will be followed by your visibility and activeness, especially your dedication to finding and connecting with the right business profiles as you desire.

There are online social communities on social media platforms, the moment you find the one you belong in and join it, then you can start "investigating" and observing the major influences there to know which one is a prospect.

One of the many ways to connect is to talk about your business and how much about it you are excited about. Through communication, you can both or all get to know each other better, and how you will be able to help each other through value addition. With the knowledge you already have about this prospective business relationship, you can create a comfortable and identifiable platform for you both to unite and make a connection.

You can talk about ideas you think will inspire or be useful to both of you. Or you can talk about the other person's business and let them know what you think of whatever it is they are doing. If you have any suggestions or remarks to make, you can go ahead and make it. By talking about the other person's business, you are showing that you are not a selfish person, but that you care about them, and that what they are doing is important, relevant and worthy of recognition.

One of the major keys to establishing a relationship anytime, anywhere, is to show interest in the other person. You are always perceived as a nice and interactive person if you are not just into yourself. If you can have good communication with someone else without always trying to make the conversation about yourself, then you may just win them over easily. This is simply because people like to know or feel like you are interested in them. So show that you are not just trying to network for the simple good of your own business, but the mutual good of your prospective professional relationship.

Connect through presenting your values, strengths, and ideas in the area of business that you are into. When making a connection for the first time, or not, but online with other professional business owners, talk about what you have in common and make sure they get to see that you can both benefit from each other and that yours is a relationship to be trusted. Try as much as you can to reflect yourself as a trustworthy person. First impressions always matter; they always give the other person the first thing to work with about you.

Gradually build trust and friendship, none of it is supposed to be forced, so don't make the mistake of expecting to achieve a relationship immediately. Usually, online networking works with as much time as physical networking. You will take your time and become acquainted, and then gradually let them get to trust you. But of course, you will have proven over time that you can be trusted. If you can build trust gradually over time, then it begins to come off easily.

ENGAGE (MAXIMIZE YOUR TIME WITH EVERY CONNECTION)

There are groups and discussions that you will find all over the internet. These are your engagement circles and platforms. Finding your engagement circle is the first step to engaging. When you find that group, you begin to engage in them to gain visibility, access, influence, and identification—Identification with your target professional relationship. Our Accelerated Global Connections Public Facebook Group is a great place to practice this.

Engaging will bring you lots of visibility and influence, so you must learn to take this very seriously. It is through engaging that you will gain enough influence to be able to make professional relationships and gain trust. Engagement is a way people get to know you, experience you, and what value you have to offer, and then helps you spread your value. In engaging, you will be found in social communities, especially as a new business person, starting conversations, joining conversations, writing comments. You will also do this by giving your own opinions— you have to be vocal and keep yourself out there where everyone in your communities can see you. Take your time to engage on other people's sites, blogs, articles, and other social forums. Through your comments and engagements, people will see and know you, so ensure you represent your business well enough by what and how you say it. Getting involved is important, but how you make this involvement is what is more important. People will perceive what kind of person you are by what you say and how you say it. This would be a reflection of what you think.

Recommendations, if there are other businesses or products and services that you know about, engaging online can also be done by referring them. This includes those businesses which have existed before yours; you must give referrals because the more referrals you give, the more visible you become, and the more others would do the same for you. Networking is not an isolation concept; for it to be networking, it must be including something beyond just you and your own business. Referrals are a good way to make the most out of a networking experience. Promote other businesses, as well. This will earn you those businesses' trust, attention, and reciprocity.

The goal is to make the most out of your time and out of each connection you make, so leverage these connections by also promoting them. Engage heavily and be very active. Look out for some opportunities that your business can fill up, and the needs that your business can meet while engaging actively online. When you meet these opportunities, take advantage and send a message, whether as an email message or as a reactive/responsive direct message. Leverage on the opportunities that these connections provide, and give your best.

Get in touch with other businesses and create a network with them, this can be your suggestive feature. When people look up these other businesses, they will also find yours. And when people look up your own business, their businesses will be found as well. This sort of collaboration benefits you and benefits your networking relationships too.

When you come by some opportunities for your business that you may not be able to meet, you can always introduce these opportunities to your group of networks and relationships. You should know that this will make you an endearing business relationship to keep, and those relationships will always be ready and willing to do the same for you.
In addition to setting up social media account profiles, you can utilize and maximize the advantages that are present in those platforms while engaging in the communities. Hashtags, for instance, hashtags are like your easy advantage when sharing your business content. On Instagram and Twitter, for example, hashtags lead you directly to a wide range of audiences. The key is just to know the right hashtags to use. You should use hashtags that are related to your content; however, some other times, you may have to include hashtags that may not directly be related to your content but are trending. That way, a wide range of people get to see your content, you will have been seen, which equals visibility, and you stand the chance of getting feedback.

Mentions, this is another advantage that will bring you some attention. One of the ways social media users sometimes draw the attention of target personalities is by mentioning them on their posts. If you are engaged on your online platforms, try mentioning people you would love to see your post/content. Very importantly, sometimes, if not all the time, you will be wrong to equal visibility or your business' reach with the comments or likes—(reactions) you get. Wait for the feedback responses, especially through direct messages.

Building the network, you want is easy; simply know what to do, how to do it, who to follow, and what to say.

CHAPTER SEVEN
LEVERAGING SOCIAL MEDIA IN NETWORKING

Making Connections in business should not always be a product of a networking event for you. You can make business connections without waiting for that, all the time. While people wait for this, you can leverage on a couple of other means to network, since this is a proven strategy for connecting your business or brand with others in the industry or even beyond, that will increase your brand reach and influence.

This connection outside networking events can be done anytime and anywhere, from the comfort of your own laptop or even mobile phone. LinkedIn provides the platform for that.

There are over 467 million people using this platform and this has totally transformed the way networking is done. Connecting with people in your industry and beyond and applying for jobs are part of the networking benefits that this professional platform offers. Apart from giving you the ability to connect with people in your industries, a major benefit is that LinkedIn helps you connect with giants in your industry and even in other industries. Of course these successful business people are people that you may not have had the opportunity of meeting one on one. LinkedIn gives you the opportunity to meet with them.

In this book, I want to show you how to network on LinkedIn and build strong relationships from scratch that will scale your business or career. After this, you will be able to navigate through networking on LinkedIn like a professional.

CREATE A UNIQUE PROFILE

First impressions matter a lot in the business of networking, whether it is a face to face physical networking or online networking. So, ensure that there is full optimization of your profile before you venture into networking on LinkedIn. Do not leave any blank spaces, ensure to fill every space in the profile section. This is because as a resume is key for those seeking jobs, your linked in profile is your resume, you need to make it look as professional as professional can be. This means that you will have to use headlines that will show people what you are doing and your areas of specialties, if there are more than one.

Professionals may not have the patience to read through your resume, paying attention to details as they ought to, so they resort to using keywords to spot those who they think are good in a required field especially in the industry they function in. This only means that if you will attract professionals to patronize you, you must learn to use keywords as that is what they are looking out for. When you incorporate the use of keywords in your headline, summary and your experience, you obviously as compared to those who do not use, have an added advantage.

Keywords are very important because if someone makes a search on LinkedIn and you used the Words in the search for your profile headline, you have chances of your profile coming up first unlike those that didn't use the search words as the keyword for their profile heading. For example, if someone searches for 'Digital Marketer" and you used "Digital Marketer" as the keyword in your headline, your profile will come up first. This alone gives you a greater opportunity with those you want to connect with you.

Make your profile picture as professional as possible, it speaks a lot about you. Profiles that have professional headshot pictures have more views and interactions than those that do not.

INTERACT AND CONNECT WITH PEOPLE

After going through the process of fully optimizing and setting up your profile in a professional manner, do not stay idle. Make sure you go ahead and start connecting with people on the platform. You will appear developed in your industry of choice when you have about 500 connections made on LinkedIn. The caution you have to apply as you make multiple connections is; do not make connections with just anybody you come across with. If you do not see yourself doing business with these people or working with such persons in that industry in the future, there is no need making the connections. So, as much as making connections are good, ensure you make the right connections. Personalize your notes and send alongside your connection requests, the notes will or should contain; a brief introduction of yourself and why you want a relationship with them, this will help them not receive you as a random individual just trying to add to the number of connections that you already have.

The ultimate goal is not to send requests and for the requests to be accepted, the main aim of networking is actually to network, to build relationships across your industry. So, once your requests have been accepted, it is not a time to relax like all your needs have been met. Remember you came to build relationships and no relationship survives without communication. To stay in constant communication with the people you have connected with, be sure to frequently visit their wall, make comments on their posts as much as you can on their pages, share their content and like them as well. You can even go as far as checking up on them from time to time by sending them a personal messages to see how they are doing. If you do not communicate your relationship will not grow.

LET THE CONTENT YOU POST BE ENGAGING

Content is that difference that separates professionals from professionals, so you have set up a professional profile, don't just sit back and relax, put up content that will inform and educate those that you are connecting with, this will make them see you as the professional that you really are. Go beyond sharing an article you read or saw on the internet, show them that you can lead the industry with your thoughts and ideas. Start putting together your articles or write ups on LinkedIn.

When you begin to share your content on LinkedIn, it will be easy for people you have not connected with to find you and it will make those you have connected with see you as an expert in your field. Hashtags are a must as you share your articles for people to see, especially when you are looking at attracting a target market of people and growing your networking influence. When you are finally a known voice on LinkedIn, networking will be easier and your comment section will be on fire, it will be good startup points for conversations.

BE PART OF GROUPS IN LINKEDIN
Joining groups on LinkedIn is a very good step towards making connections and getting heard on the platform. As you join groups, ensure you join the ones that relate to your industry. Your profile becomes visible to a lot of people in your industry and this in itself expands your reach and helps you connect to more people. If you search for Tech on LinkedIn on the group search of the platform, you can have about 12,000 groups show up and you can become a member of the whole 12,000 if you like.

The group strategy is good, but joining a group without interaction is almost like not joining at all. So, you will ensure that you interact well in the groups you have decided to join. In the group, ask questions, show you are an expert via your comments and posting of relevant content. Remember you are in a group, and a group has a lot of people in it, so you must be careful to put out content that will benefit the public in general, by doing so, you will have the interest of the group members at heart and not just yours alone. This way, you will not appear annoying to those who are members of the group.

Using LinkedIn for networking is a very good way of connecting with people in your industry and even other industries around the world. Building networks with people and those that recruit people for jobs online opens you up to a lot of opportunities online and these opportunities, when maximized, will skyrocket your business or career. If you're looking to take your LinkedIn game to an even higher level than the basics shared here. I suggest connecting with AGC member and LinkedIn Rockstar Mike O'Neil mOneil@integratedalliances.com

HOW TO NETWORK PROFESSIONALLY WITH FACEBOOK
Facebook is that platform that enables you to communicate with friends and families, share pictures and videos from your phone or laptop.

Facebook has all these interesting features, but these are not the only features that Facebook has. What Facebook can be used for goes beyond just sharing pictures with friends and family members as well as videos. Facebook has over 900 million people using it daily around the globe, and thus has made it one of the most common platforms that is so good for marketing, especially business to customer marketing. Their ads are targeted and they use the users likes and interactions to know the people that the user intends to advertise to.

Gradually, this platform is becoming a platform that offers services that are more career and professionally oriented. This is seen in the modifications and the added details that is contained in the section of the user's personal profile. Details like; information of work and education. A lot of employers know this, so they go ahead to check the profile of those they want to recruit, others can search for the people they want to recruit on Google before they actually have personal interviews with them. As they search on Google, one of the details that show up is your Facebook profile.

Facebook usage some years back by people is not the same today, this is because as the years went by, friend requests went beyond friends and families and we now have colleagues at work sending friend requests to each other, the same for managers and customers. This means that it is no longer a platform that is just for social networking. This tells you that personal branding happens on Facebook the same way it happens on LinkedIn.

We have looked at how one can use LinkedIn for networking professionally, we want to look at how one can also use Facebook.

CHANGE YOUR VANITY URL
A vanity URL is your domain on Facebook that has its own customs. So arranging this domain well is the basic thing you will have to do to create your own brand. After opening a Facebook account, your URL is basically in a default state, comprising numbers and alphabets. For example, you will have Facebook.com/3452j40ijt. So you should change it to your name. Like https://www.facebook.com/connect2travis/. Vanity URLs serve also as the email address of your own Facebook page. Just go to the profile section, then Vanity URL and change it to a customized name.

GO THROUGH YOUR PRIVACY SETTING

You now know that professionals that know you will send you friend requests, you can decide if you want them to see your videos and pictures. If you want them to see it, fine. If you do not want them to see it, then you can choose to hide it from them, you can just set up a different group where the members of that group can have access to your full profile.

USE A PROFESSIONAL PICTURE

Let the picture be like the one you use on LinkedIn, a professional headshot picture. You can decide to be unique to give your Facebook visitors a different experience on Facebook. As long and this is not going to affect your brand negatively, it is fine to go unique. Let your picture speak of the kind of person that you are, your picture is your brand representative, so make it authentic. if the picture shows that you were on the mountain, then you will be showing that you like to climb mountains or you have an experience in mountain climbing.

LET YOUR DETAILS BE PROFESSIONAL

If you check well, you will find out that professional info on people's personal profile on Facebook, has been made more obvious. This is how you will know, the first detail in your bio after your name is your job. Facebook may have taken this approach because of its professional competitor LinkedIn.

Ensure you input the name of the organization you work in as well as your job description in that company. Don't make the mistake of putting who you are, put what you do. For example, instead of saying "you are a consultant", say things like "Large scale project manager in public sectors", this description makes your job clear. Do not forget to put the school you attended as this will help your school classmates find you and this is an added advantage.

USE BRANCHOUT AS THE LINKEDIN OF FACEBOOK

Facebook has an application that is decent, it is called BranchOut and this third party is about networking professionally networking on Facebook. This third party application allows you to search for contacts, both yours and theirs, based on company. For example, if in your network, you search for people working in Microsoft, the people you find in your search can introduce you to the manager that is hiring those looking for Jobs in Microsoft. With this application called BranchOut, you can make recommendations for people. Facebook is not the only platform that has this third party application, on LinkedIn, it is called Mini-Me. Setting up BranchOut is not difficult, all you need to do is import your CV's details, your bio and your profile on LinkedIn, as well as the Job you are good at. Although this application has not really become rampant, they have more and more people joining on a daily basis with over 30 million users.

INCLUDE YOUR BLOG RSS

This is particularly for those that have blogs somewhere on the internet, whether it is your personal blog or the blog you work in or contribute to. Plug in your social RSS feed directly to your wall to make sure that your friends and those you have networked with or you want to network with see the updates you put up. This will save you time and energy of manually putting it up on your page, they will just go to your blog directly. Some people love to read blog posts.

MAKE USEFUL STATUS UPDATES PLEASE

You are trying to appear professional, do not go on posting just entertaining posts on your status, while it is good to do that once in a while, your focus should be on positioning informative and educative content on your status. The article could be about your work industry, or something that has to do with other businesses that will benefit those that are not within your industry. People do not know that, most times, what we know about your likes and what you read are the stuff that you post on your status. This is what the person that wants to employ you or someone that wants to patronize you really wants to see. This could be boring, to the friends on your network who are not really networking with you for professional reasons, but remember your goal is to appear professional to those that you are working with or connecting with. You are trying to make your personal brand more professional.

STOP PLAYING GAMES

There are a lot of games that you can play daily on Facebook and the fact that you have time to play games on Facebook makes you look unserious and also affects your brand. You will not want someone who wants to buy from you or hire you to see you as non-busy and unserious person.

PAY ATTENTION TO GROUPS AND PAGES

Although they have more online communities' features than commercial features, groups are a very good way to network on Facebook. You can share pictures, videos and links, all those within the groups will see it. You can also send emails to those who are members of the group easily. Our AGC Facebook Groups are active with professionals seeking motivation, education, relationships and new business. Join our FREE Facebook group here: https://www.facebook.com/groups/AcceleratedGlobalConnections/

There is really no difference between your page and that of Coca-Cola, the only difference is modification. These brands only set up their pages to look "not personal" or not to look like they are seeking for Jobs. It was modified for the public. Your page has all the full analytics that allow people to click and interact with you on your page.

Your page can also rank high for your name when your name is searched for and this will do a lot of benefit to your professional career, while your personal profile is kept on lockdown.

Check out the AGC Facebook Page Here: https://www.facebook.com/joinAGC/

FACEBOOK EVENTS ON FACEBOOK

On Facebook, there are good event engines that allow you to make a post and invite people. This means that you can put on an event for your industry, how you would see an evening of networking for those in your industry, people will eventually join and organize the event for and with you. The benefit of running events is that it sets you up as a leader in that field and this is useful for the success of your personal brand.

NETWORKING ON INSTAGRAM

Nothing is more important today in the world of business than building very solid online relationships. It can range from posting on Facebook, being part of a group on LinkedIn. These are ways to channel your energy put on social media platforms as you move towards business success.

You have to spend your energy on the platform where your main target market spends their time, if you must make a lot of impact through or on your social media channels. For women born in this 21st century, Instagram is the in thing, more than half of the women in this century spend time on Instagram daily, and the age range of the total number of people using Instagram(about 800 million people) are between 18 to 29 years of age. I want to show you how you will use Instagram for professional networking.

As this platform is a social media platform where most people go to find out content about friends, family, friends, influencers, celebrities and colleagues, you must take your activities there a little bit above using the platform to network professionally in a passive manner.

SLIDE INTO DMs

You may think that because people have used this term to create memes, it has taken the professional touch that comes with it, sliding into the DMs of people is of a very big advantage. Although this requires that you leave your comfort zone of waiting for people to message you, and you go ahead to start a chat with them. You may go from either their story on Instagram or replying to news feeds on their page.

You must know that if you must send a DM to someone, you would have made your research to find out what the person's feed and style is all about. You should be able to highlight this relevant information you have researched. This is what I mean; if you are talking with a fashion influencer on Instagram, you should be able to have gone through the person's videos or daily outfits on different occasions, especially the ones posted on his or her feeds. It could be about a fashion holiday, an outfit of the day. You should find out also how they communicate by paying attention to the kinds of posts they use and their most used emoji. Ensure your message to them carries their patterns of communication, this is because when you speak their language they will understand and connect with you faster. When they understand you, it makes them feel that you have taken time to pay attention to the kind of brand that they are selling.

JOIN PODS ON INSTAGRAM

In starting a one on one relationship with those you want to connect to you on Instagram, sending direct messages is good, but it is not the only way of building relationships on Instagram. Just like Facebook and LinkedIn have groups, the groups on Instagram are called pods. You can also build strong relationships by joining pods. As you join pods, you will obviously see more accounts that are like minded with yours and want to play around Instagram using "algorithm timeline" provided by Instagram. The Instagram 'algorithm timeline" is a tool Instagram uses to highlight feeds that are specialized and curated, they base their highlight on the fact that you interact more with content instead of the way the content is posted.

This means that your content must get as many likes as possible. Getting more likes and comments can be done using Instagram pods, all you do is post a link and persuade people to like and comment, make sure the content will benefit them. It may be hard at first but if you get consistent, you will not have to be too persuasive with people, they will naturally go to the link you posted because they know there is something to learn from it. As your likes and comments increase, your posts will get to the top of the feed reaching a larger audience.

A part of an Instagram pod that has female entrepreneurs that are into social media marketing is Dee Nuncio of Mod Op. Instagram pods will give you the opportunity to really socialize, you will meet different personalities having common interests as you, sharing common grounds. You will also have an added advantage of these people sharing your original high quality posts, and you will also learn from others by sharing their content.

USE HASHTAGS AGGRESSIVELY
Instagram hashtags are your highway to being known on the platform. If you want people to find you on Instagram, you will learn to use Instagram hashtags. Let your hashtags not be less than thirty on each post you make on your feed or story. Hashtags will help you gain more followers and they will trigger more engagements for you. As you do this, you will be getting more followers and you will also meet likeminded influencers.
When you want to use hashtags on your Instagram post or feeds, don't just put in any Instagram hashtags, you will have to put trending Instagram hashtags. Finding trending hashtags is not difficult, just go to the search bar and find the hashtags that are on the trending posts that are similar as yours. The trending posts are obviously the most recent posts. Just find out the hashtags that they carry. You will find accounts with few followers and those with millions of followers using the hashtags. Think thoroughly about the people that will reply more to DMs and plan strategically the way you will reach out to them. This is what to do, the

more followers influencers or individuals they have, the less likely it is that they will reply to your DMs, so do not start with them, start with micro influencers and individuals, those whose followers are between 1,000 to 10,000 followers. It has been proven that micro influencers bring more return on investments using the levels of their engagements on Instagram. Also, it is really difficult to see micro influencers that are managed by agencies, so the individuals that are micro influencers will always go back to checking their messages on Instagram, they usually run Instagram business accounts.

When you want to connect with people that are connected to brands, for example you want to connect to users connected to Coca Cola, you can use the hashtag #openhapiness. This will generate millions of Coca Cola user generated posts on Instagram. With this you can connect to Coca Cola lovers on Instagram using a simple hashtag. Simple right?

TAG FRIENDS
Instagram is a truck load of posts, both inspirational, educational and funny. These posts encourage those that view them to comment and not only comment, but also to tag friends in the comment section. Tagging friends and people is the trick a lot of brands, private users and influencers use in order to go viral and gain more people to follow them. Do not post anything and not tag friends or contacts, this is because tagging friends or contacts means you are calling them to share in the outcome that the post will bring, it can be laughter, inspiration, education or information. More than sharing an already circulating content, be it a meme or an inspiring post, you should create your own, using Canva or Adobe Spark. I personally like Canva. Whether it is a video, picture, quote or a meme, creating it yourself gives it the originality that people are looking for. This of course will delight those that are following you and those you are tagging to come and enjoy the post with you. You can create a post that will inspire the entrepreneurs titled "goals getting is achieved as you're go getting", then tag all them, as much as you can tag already existing on your network. Tag them to the actual image you made with Canva or Adobe Spark post. Learn to also give shout-outs to those you are networking with, this will bring the relationship offline. It will take it from being virtual and make it a reality.

EXPLORE SECTION AND DISCOVERY
The part of Instagram where you go to explore, opens you up to a lot of

discoveries, it is an endless list to what you can find. Remember I already said that Instagram uses an algorithm that highlights the accounts that you should be following, since they already provided this for you, it is nothing but a pool of opportunities to harness from. You have potential customers in these highlighted accounts. Engage these accounts and their content and send them a DM to kick start the relationship. Don't rush into them, you are just starting to build a relationship with them, be courteous enough to tell them who you are and how you found their accounts on Instagram.

In the world today where digitalization is the in thing, if you will grow your business or career, then strong relationships are monuments that you must build. Instagram is the platform where you can do that, by giving out valuable content to those you are networking with and those that you want to network with. As you do this, you are taking your Instagram business or business on Instagram to new heights. If you are looking for more information on how to grow your business using Facebook or Instagram ads I encourage you to reach out to AGC member Jane E Johnson as she is an expert in this area. janet@janetejohnson.com

NETWORK ON ZOOM

Zoom's has quickly become the go to video conferencing tool for professionals around the world while sheltering in place, working from home during the Covid-19 pandemic. Zoom (Zoom.us) is a very important networking tool that should not be overlooked by anyone who is serious with expanding the reach of their career and business in the digital space. This platform can help you build your network marketing provided you use it as often as possible. The advantage of zoom is that the basic features are free of charge, but with the Pro account; you can get it for as cheap as 100 dollars a year.

There are four (4) Major ways to use Zoom if you want to build your network marketing business

ENGAGING YOUR TEAM WITH ZOOM.US.

People usually have the habits of signing up for products, and sometimes not buy. They will just remain for the purpose of the community and the network of people that are in the community. This tells you that it is wise to create a community within your networking team. You can never underestimate the power of staying with people that are like-minded as you, this obviously is the reason people do not leave communities even though they do not really interact there. It will keep you positive and focused.

With Zoom, you can talk to about 50 people at a time, with payment, you can talk with even more. Not just talking, because this is a visual platform, you can see who you are talking with and record the calls. It also has features that enable you do live chats.

TRAINING YOUR TEAM

When you want to train your network marketing team, Zoom is the best option especially when the professional who will train your team is not coming down to the physical location of your company (if you have one). It will also help save training cost as there will be no need for coming to the location. It is a powerful tool, when in training, it is possible for people to see you and connect with you as a leader. Face to face interactions will always produce more passion than interactions that happen just with chats that don't allow you see the face and body language of the person speaking. As they see you and interact with you, it will create more connection and passion in the people that are being trained.

CALLING THOSE YOU ARE MENTORING WEEKLY

The people you are mentoring can now be reached with Zoom calls weekly. Especially people that just came into the world of business and you are training them weekly. As you interact with them, the connection is created because there is a visual communication and not just an audio communication that happens over a phone call. With zoom, you can make communication more effective, this is because the person you are calling will not just be hearing your voice, but will also be seeing the movements of your body. You know body language goes a long way in effective communication.

WEBINARS AND PRESENTATION OF A PRODUCT OR OPPORTUNITY

There are a lot of platforms for hosting business webinars. People still use Hangouts, for webinars that require a large number of people, and when they want the webinar to be repetitive, they use Easy Webinar. This is not really how Zoom works, with Zoom, you can really connect intimately or have very closed classes where products and opportunity can be talked about. When having these classes, there is a high level of intimacy because you can see everyone, and this alone will birth and develop an atmosphere of high success when the presentation or the webinar is done.

I know that the tips provided here are helpful when it comes to using Zoom for effective networking. Ensure to give it a try, you will be shocked how much success you will make in your business and career and how your reach will be expanded. Remember I mentioned that with the pro account you can have more, so if you want to have more time for your meeting longer than 40 minutes, you MUST upgrade to a pro account as this is only possible there.

I do roughly three to five Zoom meetings per day during the work week to stay connected to my referral partners. Using Zoom during a pandemic is equivalent to meeting at the coffee shop for a face to face meeting.

CHAPTER EIGHT
RECONNECT, ASSESS, ACTIVATE, AND MULTIPLY VALUE

We have, at some point in our lives, made a good connection with other business professionals, and have developed a genuine relationship with them. However, certain things changed, and we lost the connection we had with them. It is almost impossible not to lose touch with a contact in a constantly changing business world. You could get transferred to another branch office, launch a different business, change your residential location, or simply get a new job. When any of these things happen, it could affect the way we relate to our networks. We could lose touch with certain important connections that used to be very active. Don't get frustrated when this happens, there is always a way to get back in touch with them.

In this chapter, we will be talking about how to reconnect with those seemingly lost contacts. We will also be looking at how to assess and activate your professional network to multiply value.

HOW TO RECONNECT
Most times, it seems easier to connect with people we are meeting for the first time than with people we have once had some kind of connection with. We never want to look like we desperately need their help, so we don't even try. There is no big deal in trying to reconnect with your lost

contact. In my opinion, reconnecting with people we used to have a connection with should even be easier than building a connection with new people because there is already a connection, we just need to re awaken it. There is a memory that you can resurrect that makes the connection all the more interesting. All you have to do is to find an event or any memory at all that was the highlight of your connection in the past and start from there.

Reconnecting with old contacts is as important as building new ones. You never can tell, your next stage of advancement may depend on them.

DON'T BE AFRAID TO RECONNECT

Networking is a vital aspect of advancing as a professional. We constantly engage with people that we share a common interest with or knowledgeable folks who can broaden our horizons. This can make a major contribution to our career development and help us achieve our goals. But sometimes life happens, and after working so hard to connect with our fellow professionals, we lose touch with them. We can get reluctant about reconnecting with them because we are scared of the outcome, so we would rather not make a move. We settle for finding new connections with entirely new people. We tend to forget, however, that building new networks will probably take more time because it takes time and patience to earn people's trust. So while you are finding new connections, make sure to reconnect with those old contacts. Don't be afraid of reaching out. It could be complicated because you don't know how to set up a meeting, the angle to start from, or you are simply scared that a lot has changed in their lives. What is the worst that can happen? You could get turn downed! Make up your mind not to get disappointed with the reactions you might receive from your old contact when you try to reconnect with them. I know every person, no matter how professional they seem to have that emotional side that can break down when they are rejected. Well, what is life without risk? It's either the individual is excited to have us back in their lives, or they are not. Regardless of the outcome, we should be confident that reaching out is the right thing to do. So quit being afraid. Go and make that reconnection.

SHOW INTEREST

When you are reconnecting with an old contact, it is important to make them feel you really have an interest in them and that you are not just reconnecting because you need their help. Show genuine interest in them. Ask them how they have been and what they have been up to. People love to be listened to, so listen to what they are saying and don't act like you are in a hurry. By showing genuine interest in them, you will make them feel comfortable with you, and they will be excited to have you back in their lives.

CONNECT VIA SOCIAL MEDIA

One of the ways to reconnect with a business professional is to connect with them via social media. Social media is a great place for people who have lost touch with each other, to reconnect.

Social media statistics from 2019 show that there are 3.5 billion social media users worldwide, and this number is ever-growing. This equates to about 45% of the current population. Social media is a good place to reconnect with past business relationships. Since half of the world population is on social media, most business professionals are more than likely to be active across different social media platforms. Recent trends show that most businesses are now launching online platforms, and many professionals do most of their work online. There are different social platforms like Facebook, Instagram, Twitter, and LinkedIn that can help in your reconnection. It is better to do your research and find out which of the social platforms that they are most active on to avoid being ignored. I know it's not the easiest thing to do, but you have to do it anyway. For professional networking, LinkedIn is the best platform to connect on. LinkedIn is the most preferred connection for professionals because of its business-friendly features. You get to meet people who are engaged in different ventures and people with different skillsets and connect with them by simply sending a connection request. Twitter is also a good platform because many professionals post about their work on twitter. You can start by following them, retweeting, and commenting on their post so that you will easily get noticed. Instagram could be a great place, too, to reconnect with other professionals. You can send them a direct message, like their post, share their post and most important comment on their post. You could also tag them when you post content that you think they will find interesting. It is possible that they could have an enormous amount of followers on these platforms and have constant activity going on their page. That could make it difficult to get noticed, so you use other methods to reconnect with them if that is the case.

FIND MUTUAL CONNECTION

When reconnecting with professionals, it is important to look for a mutual connection to help make the reconnection easy. It could be a friend that you share, it could be a project or a goal. Whatever it might be, you must have something you mutually share. So let's say you have a mutual friend, you can ask the mutual friend to invite you both for lunch or dinner. You can start from there to catch up. While doing this, it's important to be genuine, so you don't portray the wrong picture. If you are not authentic, it will be noticed. Make sure your purpose for the reconnection is for all the right reasons and make it obvious. Let them know how long it has been since you last connected with them and what could have caused the loss of contact. While at dinner or lunch, make sure to talk about something that you both have an interest in.

ATTEND EVENTS

You need to be deliberate. Find out about online events they will be attending and attend. Online events are great places to meet people and exchange ideas. So you need to attend major online events if you want to reconnect with old contacts and build new connections. Do your research and find out which online events they will be attending based on their interest. For example, our AGC Talks Online Event.

This is an event that attracts people who love to network and learn together all the professionals that are involved in networking from executives, to stylists, to CEO's, to business owners, to entrepreneurs, to education lovers, etc. If they are into educational talks, then they are most likely to attend the weekly AGC talks Online Event. Attending events like this will allow you to meet them in their best mood and reconnect with them. This could also be a good time to bond and build trust.

REMIND HOW YOU KNOW EACH OTHER

The first thing to do when you are reconnecting is to remind the individual where and how you guys know each other. In doing that, be careful not to oversell or undersell. This is one major mistake that people make when they are reconnecting with lost networks. Don't assume that they will remember you (overselling), or you might sound insincere. Saying something like "I have so missed you" when you are not so sure if the person will remember you will make you look desperate and make the person wonder why you are pushing so hard. Don't assume that the person will not remember you at all (underselling). Don't say, "I know you will not remember me..." The individual might think, "oh well, if I don't know you, then why are you bothering me. Instead, you can say, "my name is Richard, I met you at XYZ during ABC." That way, you leave the "remembering part" to the individual without overselling or underselling. The person is most likely to respond positively, whether they remember you or not.

FOLLOW-UP

This is where a lot of people miss it. If you just connected with an individual after six months of losing contact with them, don't wait for another six months before you connect back. Remember building the first connection with people without any form of follow-up is a total waste of time. You don't have to go overboard by sending them flowers or sending them a long emotional message, but you can follow them up by dropping a short text to say "hello" every once in a while. You can even set up a lunch with them to deepen your connection. Just don't forget to pick up the phone and wish them well.

ASSESS AND ACTIVATE

Now that you have successfully reconnected with an old contact, you are probably wondering when would be the perfect time to assess and activate the relationship. It is always better to take things slowly. Like we discussed earlier, you do not want to sell your network the idea that the reason why you are reconnecting with them is that you need their help. You want to show them that you have a genuine interest in them and that you value the relationship.

Every professional knows how important networking is in advancing their career. We can leverage our networks to achieve our goals. Through networking, we can boost sales, increased visibility, gain relevant knowledge and experience, learn new skills, and be exposed to new opportunities. Networking has a "multiplier effect." It can help us multiply value. A network is perfect when the value generated is mutual; that is, each party is benefiting from each other's input. But leveraging your network can be dicey. In as much, your networks are there to render help to you; you must not sell the idea that you are taking advantage of them. Your goal must first be to build a genuine relationship based on trust and not for selfish reasons.

CALL FREQUENTLY

Putting a call across at the right time can be very useful. It shows you are thoughtful, that you have them at heart and that you genuinely care about them. Ensure your call is strategic, It has to be semi-formal. Your conversation should sound like this, "Good morning Jane. How are you? How is the family?" Then ask about how her latest project is going, ask her how you can help out. Talk about the most popular headlines on the news, crack some jokes, and bid her goodbye. Ensure it ends on a great note and make them feel good about themselves and what they can achieve. That call could determine what mood they are in for the rest of the day, and they will thank you for it.

SHARE SOMETHING OF VALUE WITH THEM

Professional networking is all about exchanging value with other professionals. So ensure you are always adding value to them. It is easier to assess and activate a network when they value your input. Always be willing to be of help to them. Find articles you think they will need and send it to them. Share your knowledge and experience with them. Constructively criticize their work, let them know where they are getting it wrong and where they can make amends. Offer them valuable opportunities that will advance their profession. They will value your advice, and they will constantly be looking for ways to reciprocate.

BE SUPPORTIVE

Never underestimate the power of genuine support. Everyone needs a support system. Support them in any way you can. Refer a friend to them, promote their products, and talk about their brand. Retweet their post, comment on their post, you can also share their post. Play an active, supportive role in the individual's life without being a stalker. If they launch a new product or start a business, be one of the first to patronize them. By doing this, you are earning their trust and activating the relationship.

TAKE TIME TO MAKE A REAL CONNECTION

Connect with them on a personal level. Build a relationship based on trust that extends beyond the world of business. Don't just be a business partner, be a friend. Go for walks together. Attend social online events together. Have lunch or dinner together. Let them see you as a genuine friend, and they will be more than willing to help you out when they need to. That is what friends do, after all, they help each other out.

FIND MUTUALLY BENEFICIAL GOALS

One of the easiest ways to forge a united relationship with people is to work with them towards achieving a common goal. Find ways you can work together to achieve a common goal that will be of benefit to you both. Jump at every opportunity to invest in them because the better they are, the more likely they will be of benefit to you and help you achieve your goal. They will appreciate your efforts to make them better people. If you want to achieve your goals help enough other people achieve their goals.

LEARN FROM THEM

Assessing and activating your network is not necessarily asking them for help or asking them for advice. Networking intelligently means that you should learn from your relationship with them without even asking. Watch how they do things and apply their methods to your profession. Take every opportunity to hang out with them or attend meetings that they set up. The closer you are to them, the more you will learn from them. So get close to that knowledgeable individual in your network. Watch them and learn from them.

CONNECT THEM TO OTHERS

Learn to be a master connector. Identify two individuals in your network who will be of benefit to each other, set up an online meeting with them through Zoom, and introduce them to each other. They will see you as a valuable person who has a lot of connection which can help you massively in your career. They will also want to help you meet other people in their network who can be of help to you.

ACKNOWLEDGE THEM

People love it when others acknowledge them for their works. You can use this to your advantage. Always find an opportunity to acknowledge them. Send them acknowledgment letters or emails once in a while. If you have a network that offers you quality value, then you will be doing yourself more harm than good if you fail to acknowledge them. When they hit a career milestone or get promoted at their place of work, acknowledge it. When they launch amazing products or hit record sales, acknowledge it. Send them a simple congratulatory message and let them know that you are happy for them. My friend Bo Young is a master at this and he has a great service through Banner Season to streamline this process. Connect with him for more information. thelbm5@me.com

BE A MOTIVATOR

Every individual needs a motivator. Motivators are very much appreciated. We all experience downtimes when we need someone to tell us that we are good enough, that we can achieve whatever we want to achieve, and that we can become whoever we want to become. Someone who has walked down the road we are currently walking on and who conquered it. When we look at such people, we know we can do it too. Find every opportunity to motivate your network with uplifting words. If you have experienced what they are currently experiencing, let them know, and suggest solutions to them. Inspire them through your actions. Encourage them to never give up. Be there when they need someone to talk to. They will trust you and will find a way to reciprocate.

ASK, AND YOU WILL RECEIVE

When you are ready to ask your network for help, don't hesitate. This is where a lot of professionals get stuck. They are either too humble or too proud to ask. It could be that they are scared of being turned down. Whatever the reason it might be, you will never get anything out of your network if you fail to ask. Whether you need to raise capital to run a business or finance a project, you need knowledge from an experienced individual, or you want to partner with an individual who has the required skill to achieve an objective, just go ahead and ask. Don't expect people to assume you need their help. Some people might ask you how they might help you, but you can't bank on that. The worst answer you can ever get is a "no," and it doesn't hurt. If you get turned down on your first attempt, don't be discouraged from making a second attempt. Be valuable to your network. If you are truly valuable to your network, it will be difficult for them to turn you down when you ask for their help.

CHAPTER NINE
THE POWER OF LEVERAGING YOUR NETWORKS FOR BUSINESS

The first thing that comes to mind when we hear the word "networking" is a picture of forced conversations and handshakes with strangers at a conference meeting or events, which is particularly normal. Building networks is more than just exchanging business cards and adding another connection to your LinkedIn account. It is about how work gets done in our complex and interconnected business environment, where building and sustaining a diverse array of network relationships is a key element of effective leadership.

However, one of the most important endeavours for our professional growth and success is also one of the most confusing and intimidating for many people, if not most. Starting from introverts, who find it difficult to put themselves out into the world in a bigger way. To those who are scared to meet new people online or in person, to individuals who have not yet understood the power of personal branding.

There are thousands of professionals neglecting the need to network, and turning their backs on opportunities that could have changed the course of their careers. 70% of job openings are not listed, and the only way one can get to them, is through networking, it is very clear that your network, that is your community of trusted and supportive colleagues, clients, partners, peers, former and current managers who are excited to speak for you and your excellent capabilities, they are the exact people that will open doors for you and unlock amazing opportunities for you, that you simply might not have access to without their help.

In this world, where technology has become the conduit for a network, especially social media platforms such as Facebook, Twitter, Instagram, Telegram, Zoom, and so many more, there is no telling how much work one can get done.

It is said that the richest people in the world look for and build networks, everyone else looks for work. It is quite shocking that so many individuals do not see these social platforms as a means to build their network.

Looking at today's society, the importance of acquiring social skills play a great role in realizing one's true potential both as an individual and as a professional. Now among these key skills, there is no doubt that networking stands out because no matter what one wants to accomplish, most of the time, it involves dealing with several other people who can make it happen. The skill can come in more useful for a startup founder since they will need to deal with the possible stakeholders in the system; they are customers, investors, mentors, vendors, and so many others, to bring his or her vision to life.

Now, this does not just get you noticed in the crowd, it also can fast track your road to success if it is effectively harnessed. So making things click for a business is dependent on how you leverage the right connections at the right time. So if you do not have the right connections, it might be frustrating trying to get things done.

Now the annoyance of many service professionals is that, although they might despise networking, it is of utmost importance that they grow their business. There are good lawyers, accountants, real estate agents, and consultants, for example, that often feel that their excellent work for clients alone should bring a constant flow of solid referrals.

The truth is, it does not always work like that, it might work for some people and their businesses but mostly not every business. Your clients are busy, so they will not always remember you when someone in their network needs what you have to offer. And even if they remember you and they go as far as keeping you at the top of their mind, the thing is their network also is limited. Some strategies help in getting exciting new roles meet sponsors and mentors, they also help in achieving higher accomplishments and bring new opportunities that will elevate and inspire individuals to do their best and greatest works.

They also help in developing a stronger entrepreneurial mindset and approach to a person's career growth, which is something that is much required today, whether the person is in a corporate role or their own venture. So here is how to network up successfully.

HANGING OUT WHERE SUCCESSFUL PEOPLE ARE

Ever heard the saying, "you are addressed the way you are dressed? Truthfully that is true because people will always address you the way you present yourself. If you want to be successful, you might want to begin to act and see yourself as successful, probably change the group you hang around with. If you want to be successful and the only people you hang around with are those that do not challenge your mental growth, you will be seen as unserious. Now we are all different at our place of career, so you start by assessing the place you are and then determine where you can go to network.

EMBRACING DISCOMFORT

The thing about being comfortable is that it can be very tricky. To network takes a lot more than just being in your comfort zone and waiting for everything to happen just like that. It is like waiting for a baby to fall from the sky without any effort whatsoever. Your business is that baby that needs nurturing so that it can grow. If you do not put any effort in providing the needs of that baby, it might not grow as healthy as you want it to.

So if you are not uncomfortable connecting with someone, then you are not aiming high enough. You will need to get past your comfort zone and go talk to them. Your discomfort may be a sign that you are talking to the right person. This is another reason I started AGC Accelerated Global Connections. I was seeing over and over again people getting too comfortable in their lateral networks and not aiming to raise the quality of their network. You will never see the executive or CEO of a major company sitting in a weekly network meeting however they love to attend high quality events with tons of people where they can come and go as they please.

DO NOT SELL OR PITCH TO THEM

Selling or pitching to a person, that you are networking with for the first time is wrong. Some people do this wrong. Everyone comes to a networking event with something to sell but no one came there to buy.

DO NOT BUY INTO THE IDEA THAT INTROVERTS CANNOT NETWORK.

This ideology is not entirely true, because introverts can play to their strengths by inviting people for one on one coffee, they can also host small dinner gatherings or even networking by writing blog posts and attracting others to them online.

All of those strategies are less emotionally stressful than having to go up to strangers and talk to them. I am an introvert by nature but I understand the importance of networking up and have trained myself to be more extroverted to have success in networking.

YOUR NETWORKING EFFORTS SHOULD BE FOCUSED IN THE RIGHT PLACES.

It can be frustrating and also be a waste of time when you invest or take action in the wrong places. You can work in a room for as long as you want, but what good would it be if you are in the wrong room to start with.

You would have to identify the right ecosystem for your needs. If you want to start a software company, you would have to identify the major players in Silicon Valley.

BE THE KIND OF PERSON THAT IS REWARDING TO MENTOR.

Now mentoring people can be very difficult. Leading people is one of the most difficult thing one can do, so before you decide to turn yourself in for mentorship, you have to consider some things.

First of all, you have to ask yourself questions like, would I like to mentor myself? Am I open, flexible, and resilient? Am I eager to learn and committed to modifying how I am going to interact with the world, so I can have more success, reward, and happiness?

Some steps can be taken to ensure that you become a great mentee and protégée who will attract more support.

Be good at what you do: This might sound very obvious, but it is the most important thing that you can do to get noticed.

Ask for more responsibility: asking for more responsibility can be the best way to show how capable you are. You have to have specific ideas for how you can contribute in a deeper, more expansive way. Being creative and outside the box.

Do not be an onlooker: do not be a wallflower; participating in all meetings, even optional ones, can be very beneficial. You can volunteer to represent your team on important department initiatives.

PROMOTE THE SUCCESS OF OTHERS
Being generous and open is very critical to your success, and the truth is, it will always be remembered. No one ever forgets the good that has been done for them; at the same time, people love people who are accountable, and have nothing to hide.

Build your internal and external support network: to succeed, you have to help others to succeed. So what you do is, you reach out to groups within your company and outside your line of business. Learn what they do and how you can help them succeed.

THE NEED FOR CONSTRUCTIVE FEEDBACK
People will not always know that you need help, if you do not show or tell them, they assume you are fine. If you shy away from asking for assistance or support. This Is very common amongst professionals, they find it extremely hard to identify and articulate what they want clearly and also the boldness to go ask for it.

This may be for fear of being embarrassed that we are not there, the fear of looking inferior, and the reluctance to appear vulnerable. A lack of inner worthiness to believe we deserve help.

You have to know that individuals, professionals and their service firms grow when they find constructive ways to leverage and expand their networks for the development of their businesses.

Now talking about leveraging, if we go by the dictionary meaning of "leverage," it is the ability to earn very high returns when operating at a high capacity utilization of a facility. A lot of people do not know how to leverage or utilize their networks to start-up their business or even expand an already existing one.

Business owners or rather, individuals do not know the power of leveraging their networks. They think networking is by luck, and so they treat it that way. They do not know that some simple planning they can increase their chances of success.

So to understand the power of leveraging, here are some steps to follow and to do this you have to first;

DEFINE YOUR GOALS
The idea that your business is going to grow without proper planning is a very ridiculous one. Removing that idea would be a very good place to start. Networking takes time to build, so if you think that the business goals you set would be met within the next three months through networking, you would have to go back to your drawing board, because these goals are unrealistic. Networking is a long-term approach.

What you do is to list out two primary goals for the next three months to six months, and then two secondary goals, that you foresee being priority in the next six to twelve months.

IDENTIFY YOUR TARGET MARKET
Networking has to be deliberate and not left to happenstance, this means that you would have to identify people/organizations you want to build a strong networking relationship with. You have to go narrow and deep; that way, you would find out who makes the purchasing or partnership decisions at the companies you set out to partner or network with. The good thing with this, you will always find every information you need by checking the speaker roster from industry events, corporate press releases, and maybe LinkedIn. So whatever you do, try focusing your arrow to the precise target or else you might miss the opportunity.

IDENTIFY YOUR "STRATEGIC CONTACTS."
Now you might ask, why do I need to be strategic finding my contacts? As mentioned earlier, finding the right target market may just be the right thing to do. In a world where social media is prevalent, there is

almost no excuse for unwanted calls and emails anymore.

Mark Suster once said, "In the era of social networks, if you cannot figure out how to get access to your venture capitalist, hang up your cleats now.

However, it is very important to know how to identify your strategic contacts. Now, these contacts are the ones who can provide introductions to your target market, and creating a list of them is with LinkedIn. Also when you are searching, there are some things you have to keep in mind; When you search, you have to scroll through the contacts of those who appear, you will find out that there are companies and positions that you never thought existed.

Once you find the search that works best for you, saving it would be a smart move to make, just in case you might need it in the future.

EMAIL YOUR STRATEGIC CONTACTS
Since you now have your list of strategic contacts, you begin your outreach through your email, which would have to come in two parts, they are;

CREATING VALUE:
This is one of the rules of marketing, if you can create value before asking for it in return, it is a very good starting point to leveraging your network. This is doubly true for networking, and it does not require a lot of effort. Just a little gesture to a strategic contact can pay a large dividend.

Like the examples below:
You provide an unsolicited intro to somebody in the same industry or company. You two might want to engage in something that interests both parties.

You might send a link to an interesting article about their industry, you could let them know how interesting, you think the article is since you have been in the industry for a while.
You could check in on how they are doing. However, whatever you do, just ensure that you provide value, give quick responses, and ensure that the conversation keeps going.

NEXT, YOU HAVE WHAT IS CALLED "THE ASK":

Now, after you have provided value for some time, you now have the opportunity to ask your contact to introduce you to your target market contact. You have to keep the communication within the previous email stream and send a simple two-sentence email. One sentence would be on your company and what you want. The other sentence on the intro, which includes a mechanism to make the intro feel natural. There are other ways to leverage your network

SECURE BUSINESS REFERRALS.

Now 88% of buyers seek advice from their connections when making purchases. So maintaining a large network not only lets you hear from people who would benefit from your company's offerings, but it would also create a lot of opportunities to ask for introductions from other people who you would like to support.

Your current group of happy clients and close friends will generally remember you when they are in conversations and discover that someone needs your service.

So if you can find an active way to continually remind them why your service is valuable and for whom, then they will be much more excited in their endorsement. Others will be confident about your second-degree connections and even remember your name and send referrals your way.

BUILDING YOUR THOUGHT LEADERSHIP

Credibility is a currency in today's economy, and the more of a thought leader you become, the greater your ability to grow your business and access other opportunities.

However, the challenge is that thought leadership has gained popularity, it has become increasingly difficult to prove authenticity and stand out in the one zillion people out there.

Nurturing and maintaining a large network that will share and engage with your content gives you the social proof needed to attract more followers and earn more business.

Now to keep your connections engaged, you will have to create content that has a mix of your expertise and that of other influential members in your network. This prevents you from coming across as too promotional, but it encourages your connections to reciprocate by sharing content. Heads up, though, an easy way to promote or boost your content engine, is to quote your connections. They will then see the need to actively share your work and return the favor by quoting you.

EXCHANGING EXPERTISE
One of the most valuable benefits of maintaining a diverse network is that it offers you perspective and advice you will not get in your office. Sometimes when you are struggling with difficult challenges or trying to decide whether or not to move from one direction to another with your business, asking external connections might be the best way to get those valuable insights.

Why would you do this? Your professional connections are not clouded by their emotional attachment to the way things currently are and can provide a different perspective from their experience in the industry, unlike the people in your company.

Do not ever think that asking people for help burdens them, especially if they do not say so. Naturally, people love sharing their expertise. Seeking their knowledge will only bring them closer to you and make them more invested in your success.

Asking for help can lead to a virtuous cycle where they will want to help you even more if handled well. The cycle is started by you taking care of them and not just thanking them, but also let them know in detail when their advice positively impacts you. Feedback is necessary.

FINDING THE HIGHEST QUALITY VENDORS
Now his may sound too ambitious, but the truth is choosing the right vendors has a significant impact on your bottom line. Even though you can find online reviews for most products, it can be quite challenging to find opinions about professional services providers. This is where your network comes in.

Ask your network about the vendors they work with. They will give you a general sense of what companies are valuable, a waste of resources, and worthy depending on what specific services you need.
Choosing vendors who share your values and with whom you enjoy

working with has a positive network effect. You will share referrals more and very easily. You will also find opportunities to share content development, and also find opportunities to partner.

CHAPTER TEN
MAINTAINING HEALTHY BUSINESS RELATIONSHIPS

Business relationships are the bedrock of every establishment. This involves whatever interaction an establishment and its employees have with other people that are outside the company, i.e. Individuals that do not constitute the workforce of the establishment of other businesses. Creating business relationships is no piece of cake, building strong bones, and making them last is even harder and requires a lot of effort on your part.

The broad classification of business relationships is identified as B2b and B2c. These are just simple acronyms that stand for Business to Business and Business to Consumers.

Business to Business: These involve all interactions you have with people in your company's vertical chain. I.e. Your suppliers down to your retailers or horizontal chain, i.e. Partnerships with other establishments and far range competitors, if you may.

Business to Consumers: Relationships here relate to that which exists between your company and your direct customers, such as is the case in hospitals or financial institutions.

Whichever be the case, or whichever business relationship is under consideration, care must be taken to ensure that a good business relationship is maintained. A good business relationship does a lot for you apart from keeping your customers and partners with your company. The greatest resource of all is the human resource. Even if you were to go bankrupt, great business relationships leave you with something to fall back on.

In this chapter, let us run a specific analysis of the different skills and helpful tips that would ensure you maintain top-notch co-existence with your business networks. These guides are not streamlined to certain kinds of companies, they are generally provided to guide every establishment in this.

The first thing you must do is to see the business relationship as just any other relationship you get into daily, most basically, your relationship with a friend or your partner. The only difference is in the level of intimacy. Business relationships are more formal and cordial than the rest but demand almost similar responsibilities on your part. Responsibilities such as devotion, commitment, loyalty, building trust, reliability, and value for each other. Jealousy and romantic feelings are, however, not included.

WORK ON YOURSELF, BE AUTHENTIC: Be yourself, but at the same time, be the best someone would want to opt for. You must be careful not to create the wrong persona, your first point of selecting networks should be identifying people and companies you share a mutual interest, goal, and vision with. This will make your Communication easier. Do not paint a picture of what your company can't offer. Just as much as you want your networks to be pleased, do not promise what you cannot deliver. False expectations are poisonous to healthy business relationships.

STAY IN COMMUNICATION: A survey was conducted of heads of companies and most entrepreneurs to reveal how many of them kept close Communication with the people they do business with; suppliers, buyers, partners, and the likes. It was discovered that a lot of these business heads most times only contact these people when they require their services. A lot of them were also discovered to have lost a lot of networks over the years. This is no surprise at all. The business environment notwithstanding, every individual you make transactions with is a human being. Like all human beings, they want to know you care beyond business matters. When they have issues, they want to know you are empathetic towards their down moments.

As often as you can afford to, maintain good communication with all within your reach. If they are the ones you can be socially active with, then, by all means, keep a conversation going there. If you have their emails alone or business cards, be sure to text or call from time to time. Help them warm up to you.

Loyalty keeps your business relationships stronger than ever; strive to achieve this. Get them loyal to you, and they will always be there when you need them.

Staying on people includes insisting they are the ones despite faulting views about them. Accept the people you connect with the way they are. Just as we have different body specifications, we also have different traits and characters that make us different from the rest. Be sure that at some point, you will encounter networks that are very difficult to relate with. Some of them even barely give you attention at the very first formal introduction. Breakthrough their walls and penetrate smoothly, leaving no stone unturned. Watch the scenery of a person threatening to withdraw their funds from a financial institution and moving it all to a different one even when they have barely been offended, see how the institution rallies around and does everything to make them stay, is it really because they are the only existent customer loyal to their bank? The process of staying through to get these networks loyal to you and willing to serve in their capacity is a tedious and slightly lengthy one and requires a lot of patience and understanding.

BE A PERSON/BRAND THEY CAN TRUST: How good are you at what you do? How greatly can I trust you to deliver at any pace or rate? Can I trust the efficacy and quality of your work? These are the concerns of individuals you have business dealings with.

They want a brand that can give them what they want as they want it and when they want it. Never take advantage of your business relationships or give them the idea that you intend to. This will turn their hearts and minds against you.

The greatest business secret of successful businesses is honesty and integrity. They want to know they can rely on you that you would forgo your interests for theirs and won't make decisions to their detriment.

Consistency further builds their trust in you; how consistent the quality of your work has been, how you respond to deadlines, to what extent you can go to achieve excellence. Build your business on the right principles, have your workers equally apply these principles, and do not hesitate to make amends for times when you get it wrong.

OFFER VALUE BEFORE YOU DEMAND VALUE: Assuming I am another business or company executive, and you approach me for certain unprecedented favors, the first rational question I would ask is this; "What do we stand to gain from this? Every business relationship operates under the simple rule of "give and take." It is simple; if I am going to assist you in this way, you've got to assist me in some way too, unless, of course, it is a non-profit or a charity organization seeking to assist businesses bloom.

Whatever offer you propose must have at its center what you can offer to the second party. Business relationships, most of the time, could be likened to investments. Just as investments are meant to yield returns, the same as business relationships. You make these networks for the growth of your business, growth should not be one-sided. As much as you wish to expand your business, they need something similar.

This is the same in mutual friendships and Relationships. I would refer to the biological term; symbiosis, in this biological relationship, both the host and the symbiont benefits from each other. Be a symbiont and not a parasite.

ASK FOR FEEDBACK: Feedback is very crucial; you want to know the areas you're failing on. No person is an island. In most cases, we do our best to be the best, but because we are not perfect, we fail sometimes and may not know it.

Feedback is the most important form of Business to Customer business relationships. You want to know how your product is faring in the market and what people have to say about it.
Even as an establishment just offering services, you want to know

how commendable the quality of your service has been, what is the experience of your customers every day they come into your business? Most companies get to know this through social media platforms, market interactions with their retailers, through feedback sheets at office receptions, and even through calls or online reviews. It is not an uncommon occurrence to have gotten such Feedback calls from our financial institutions. They do this from time to time to ensure their customers are pleased with the services they render, and they are patient through each call. They listen and let you talk. They do not get all defensive; neither do they let their emotions cloud their senses.

GIVE WEIGHT TO THEIR OPINIONS: it is not just enough to ask for feedback, what you do with the feedback given is more important at any point. See it this way; it's no use asking me the things you do that I do not like when you just keep doing the same thing.

Successful businesses thrive a lot on customer and buyer's feedback. In feedback, your customers and buyers bring to your attention the things they do not like about your product and brand and give opinions on what could be done to make it better suited for them.

Sometimes, this feedback could be irrational and inapplicable, true. Especially considering a lot of factors like finance, and production costs. Not minding how irrational this feedback could be, there's always room for compromise. Weigh the issues they laid down, critically analyse what their fears are, and make necessary adjustments that would not be a loss to both parties. The same applies to partnerships and other business networks.

GET MORE PERSONAL: Interact with your networks on a person to person basis. Get to show more interest in them. This is most times argued to be a wrong line of action because it is said to breed unprecedented emotional entanglements eventually, which isn't advised in a business relationship.

Business relationships, when defined, pose no problem at all. Getting more personal with your network does not get you to prying in their intimate private life or making Insinuations of interests other than business. This is a lot of case scenarios that have destroyed very profiting and proficient relationships.

Getting personal with your networks should involve sincere care about matters bordering on enhancing the profitability of their company and personal matters that they choose to share with you. The littlest things such as; inviting them to coffee, being open to observe when they have an unusual or different outlook from what you know them for, offering your help in matters you can assist them with, go a long way to speak volumes of the sincerity of your heart.

Be sure to remember whatever they say, including their names, even after the first hour of the meeting. Share experiences, ideas, goals, and do not be scared to show your vulnerability once in a while. This rate of interaction, however, is to just a select few, and you must be careful not to reveal too much, much more than you ought to.

NETWORK SHARING: Do not hesitate to share networks you think will be useful to your business relationships. You have different networks useful to you in diverse ways. You should introduce these networks to one another, especially when you know they would be of mutual benefit to one another.

This lighter term is called "Business match-making." Doing this will get their hearts sold on you and get them willing to do a great deal for you. However, do this one at a time; do not introduce all at once, introduce by twos according to how relevant you think they would be to each other. Besides networks you already have, be intentional about looking out for networks that could be beneficial to those you know. When you go to social events or other likes, and you get introduced to a network that is not beneficial to your business, do not be in haste to discard them. Consider if they are useful networks to the people you work with and make the connections eventually if they are.

This act of solidarity strengthens your business relationships a great deal and leaves your networks with a feeling of indebtedness towards you. They will not be in a hurry to jump to a competitive company regardless of how good the offer may be.

Do not Overdo It: As much as you would want to keep your networks blooming and healthy, you must be careful not to become a bother on their sanity. Your networks have other networks that may demand their time too, give them space to breathe, and do other things.

Do not create engagements or meetings all the time when they're not necessary. Keep in touch at a rational pace. Do not send dozens of emails and phone calls all at the same time. Have a specified time frame for that; it could be 2-3 week intervals, then occasional coffee time at both your convenience.

Learn not to demand too much too, you have many networks so the help they can supply can be diversified, learn not to overburden them with all of your company's issues. Networks are to provide assistance and help promote and better the market view of the company. Make sure you ask for just as much help as you offer.

CONGRATULATORY NOTES/BE AVAILABLE:
Do not hesitate to send congratulatory Notes over when you hear of your network's latest milestone or achievements. They should know that you always have their backs. Also, ask questions about the change and how it's helped their business. This also gives you time to catch up on other matters.

Congratulatory Notes could be sent via email or direct phone contacts depending on how you usually communicate with the partners in question. Congratulatory Notes can also be sent for personal milestones such as Marriages, birthdays, etc.

Learn to be available; your networks at some point may hand you invitations to formal events, whether formal or Informal, do your best to honor invitations. Whether it is a business conference, launch, or something as trivial as a welcome back party for a family member, make yourself available, and show your support. It could be avenues to make further connections and meet new networks.

Once in a while, besides tea or coffee, invite them to do something fun. You could play tennis together, golf, or basketball. It could equally be a party at a friend's or a club during the weekend. More than a business network, be a friend, be accessible.

Do not let Disagreements Linger: in every business relationship, just as is with all virtual and physical Relationships, disagreements must come in. Disagreements could be on financial matters, conflict of interests and views; no two people can have the same view about a matter all the time.

This is how you handle disagreements; first, see the reason for a resolution. Do not let your pride set in, two wrongs never make a right. Make the first move; call for a resolution.

The best way would be to schedule a meeting with all parties involved in a room. Consequently, everyone would be allowed to air his or her views and speak out their case. This helps to arrive at a unified cause of conflict and also clear misunderstood actions. Eventually, a compromise is reached to suit both parties. As long as the network is a meaningful one to you, you must be willing at all times to compromise even if you think you are right and they are wrong.

However, if, for some reason, you need to as a matter of fact, let go of some networks, be careful not to make enemies. Do it in the most amicable means possible. Whatever happens, ensure you did your best to keep the relationship going. Try not to burn bridges.

The usefulness of networks to any business cannot be overemphasized, thereby giving reason to the writing of this book. The sole purpose of this book is to educate the average business person on matters relating to the development of networks ranging from person to person interactions and social media connections, including its maintenance. Social media has further brought these connections home; it has created an easier platform to connect with relevant networks and has made seemingly difficult networks easily accessible. The acquisition of relevant networks can sky-rocket your business from mini to max. in a very little time frame and is the edge you have over the business that began the same time you did.

A careful study of top companies in the business world today would show personal or business relationships in high places and the very little businesses staying below the radar. Networking is a vast linkage system; the low seek the high, the high seek the higher, the chain follows that format. Having Mentors often times are also a great excuse to flex the muscles of strong networks. In seeking mentors, you seek Business professionals ahead of you, most likely either in the same or indifferent but relatable businesses as yours. These individuals have already built strong networks over the years that have enabled them to get to the point at which they stand. As time goes by, they will let you in not just on certain business secrets, but introduce you to meaningful networks that would help grow your business.

Your bank of networks should just be as strong as your will to succeed and your financial stability. This book has identified virtually all you need to build strong and long-lasting networks; the ball now lies in your court; the decision is yours to make, and the step is only yours to take. You could either decide to begin building strong networks today or limit your business abilities. Always remember; the world of business today is all about meeting the right people; people are your fastest ladders to your business success. Get climbing now!!

In a world under crisis, uncertainty, and during a pandemic people are still doing business. The answers haven't changed. You still need to build relationships, gain trust, pass quality referrals and do more business with your networks. Networking is the key, it always has been and always will be. The way we connect may have changed you may be in less in person rooms and in more online rooms but stay networking.
If you are looking for a strong network to insulate your business and recession proof your efforts, I invite you to check out AGC Accelerated Global Connections. We are a high-quality community of business professionals that love to learn together, be motivated together, pass quality referrals resulting in more business for each other. We connect and help each other at in person and online events that are accessible from anywhere in the world. We are a community network with a global impact. Find us at www.joinAGC.com